Billb

TOP 1000

SINGLES

D0869639

1955 1996

Portions of the *Billboard* chart material in this work were constructed by *Billboard* magazine from information provided by Broadcast Data Systems (BDS), which electronically monitors actual radio airplay, and Soundscan, Inc., which electronically collects Point of Sale information from music retail outlets.

HAL•LEONARD®
CORPORATION

7777 W. BLUEMOUND RD. P.O. BOX 13819 MILWAUKEE, WI 53213

CONTENTS

isplayed throughout this book are pictures of the original sheet music covers of hits nked within the Top 1000.

AUTHOR'S NOTE

Close to 22,000 songs have appeared on *Billboard* magazine's pop singles charts in the 42 years of the rock era. The titles on the following pages have spent the most time within the upper reaches of the charts, achieving their lofty status through the record, cassette, and CD purchases and radio requests from music fans.

An entertaining way of assembling these huge hits is with a ranking. There are many ways of constructing rankings. I have always premised my rankings over the years on the most-quoted statistic of a song's life on the charts, the peak position. It is where a song ultimately "placed" in the fiercely competitive race to the top of the charts.

A study of the Top 1000 hits can impart many insights on the history of *Billboard's* charts. Here are a few observations:

- In the past three years, 16 new titles now rank within the Top 100! (This illustrates the impact of *Billboard's* recent revised chart compilation methods to the "Hot 100.")
- In his first four years on the pop charts, Elvis Presley recorded 10 of the all-time Top 100 ranked hits!
- Boyz II Men, in their first five years on the "Hot 100," contributed three of the Top 5 hits of all time!
- The recent dance sensation "Macarena" far surpassed "The Twist" in weeks at #1 and weeks on the chart to become the second biggest hit ever. Yet, the '60s dance craze still counts more weeks in the Top 10 of the "Hot 100."

These are only four of thousands of insights waiting in the pages ahead. Read on and you'll discover more about America's all-time greatest hits.

Joel Whitburn

THE RANKING SYSTEM

All chart data is compiled from *Billboard* magazine's pop singles charts. See the graph below for a breakdown of those charts.

Our ranking methodology is based on the most quoted of all chart statistics, the peak position. Basically, the highest position a song title achieved on the charts determines its final ranking.

Following is the ranking formula:

1) All titles peaking at #1 are listed first, followed by titles peaking at #2, and s on.

2) Ties among each highest position grouping are broken in the following orde

    a) Total weeks title held its peak position
    b) Total weeks charted in the Top 10
    c) Total weeks charted in the Top 40
    d) Total weeks charted

If ties still existed, a computerized inverse point system calculated a point total for each title based on its weekly chart positions. For each week that a title appeared o the charts, it earned points according to each of its weekly chart positions (#1=100, #2=99 points, etc.). The sum of these points broke any remaining ties.

Below is a synopsis of *Billboard* magazine's pop singles charts, researched from th first year of the rock era, 1955. For a title that appeared on more than one of the multiple charts (Juke Box, Best Sellers, Jockeys or Top 100), its peak position is from the chart on which it peaked the highest.

DATE	CHART	POSITIONS
1/1/55– 6/17/57 (final chart)	MOST PLAYED JUKE BOX RECORDS	15-30
1/1/55– 10/13/58 (final chart)	BEST SELLERS IN STORES	20-50
1/1/55– 7/28/58 (final chart)	MOST PLAYED BY JOCKEYS	15-30
11/12/55– 7/28/58 (final chart)	TOP 100	100
8/4/58 (first chart)	HOT 100 First, all-encompassing chart.	100
11/30/91	HOT 100 *Billboard* began using actual monitored airplay (from Broadcast DataSystems), actual sales figures (from SoundScan) and playlists from small-market radio stations to compile the chart.	100

THE RANKING

hese are the Top 1000 hits that peaked on *Billboard* magazine's pop singles charts
om January 1, 1955 through September 28, 1996. (Previous editions began with
uly 9, 1955, the peak date of the first #1 rock 'n' roll hit, "Rock Around The Clock.")
Love You Always Forever" by Donna Lewis is the only record in the Top 1000 that
as still on the *Hot 100* (position #45 and falling) as of March 29, 1997; although the
ong's total weeks charted may increase slightly, its rank will remain the same.

he beginning and ending rank numbers of each page are listed on the upper out-
de corner of the page.

eep track of the Top 1000 hits in your collection by checking off the small circle in
ont of the titles.

he **PEAK POSITION** and the **PEAK WEEKS** (total weeks at peak position) are
ghlighted above the corresponding titles.

olumnar headings show the following data:

YR:	Year title reached its peak position

WEEKS:	**10** -	Total weeks charted in the Top 10
	40 -	Total weeks charted in the Top 40
	CH -	Total weeks charted

RANK:	Top 1000 ranking (highlighted in dark type)

GOLD: ● - RIAA-certified gold single
▲ - RIAA-certified platinum single (a number following the triangle indicates additional million units sold)

The Recording Industry Association of America (RIAA) began certifying gold singles in 1958 and platinum singles in 1976. From 1958 through 1988, RIAA required sales of one million units for a gold single and two million units for a platinum single. As of January 1, 1989, RIAA lowered the certification requirements for gold singles to sales of 500,000 units and for platinum to one million units. Some record companies have never requested RIAA certifications for their hits. To fill in the gap prior to 1958, other trade publications and reports were consulted.

SYM   (Symbol for type of recording):
[C] Comedy   [I] Instrumental   [S] Spoken word
[F] Foreign language   [N] Novelty   [X] Christmas

TIME:	Playing time of each title

YR	WEEKS			RANK	G O L D	PEAK POSITION	PEAK WEEKS	S Y M	TIME	ARTIST
	CH	40	10							
						Pos 1 16 Wks				
95	27	26	19	1	O	▲² One Sweet Day			4:42	Mariah Carey & Boyz II Men
						Pos 1 14 Wks				
96	60	37	23	2	O	▲⁴ Macarena (bayside boys mix) [F]			3:54	Los Del Rio
94	33	31	22	3	O	▲ I'll Make Love To You			3:58	Boyz II Men
92	26	24	16	4	O	▲⁴ I Will Always Love You			4:32	Whitney Houston
						Pos 1 13 Wks				
92	32	28	19	5	O	▲ End of the Road			5:50	Boyz II Men
						Pos 1 11 Wks				
56	28	24	21	6	O	▲³ Don't Be Cruel /			2:03	Elvis Presley
56				7	O	▲³ Hound Dog			2:15	Elvis Presley
94	30	26	18	8	O	▲ I Swear			4:15	All-4-One
						Pos 1 10 Wks				
55	26	26	20	9	O	● Cherry Pink And Apple Blossom White [I]			2:56	Perez Prado & His Orch.
55	21	21	18	10	O	● Sincerely			2:54	The McGuire Sisters
56	26	22	17	11	O	● Singing The Blues			2:23	Guy Mitchell
81	26	21	15	12	O	▲ Physical			3:43	Olivia Newton-John
77	25	21	14	13	O	▲ You Light Up My Life			3:35	Debby Boone
						Pos 1 9 Wks				
59	26	22	16	14	O	● Mack The Knife			3:04	Bobby Darin
57	30	22	15	15	O	▲² All Shook Up			1:58	Elvis Presley
81	26	20	14	16	O	● Bette Davis Eyes			3:47	Kim Carnes
68	19	19	14	17	O	● Hey Jude			7:11	The Beatles
81	27	19	13	18	O	▲ Endless Love			4:26	Diana Ross & Lionel Richie
60	21	17	12	19	O	● The Theme From "A Summer Place" [I]			2:24	Percy Faith & His Orch.
						Pos 1 8 Wks				
55	38	25	19	20	O	● (We're Gonna) Rock Around The Clock			2:08	Bill Haley & His Comets
95	25	23	16	21	O	▲² Fantasy			4:03	Mariah Carey
56	37	22	16	22	O	● The Wayward Wind			2:56	Gogi Grant
55	22	19	16	23	O	● Sixteen Tons			2:34	"Tennessee" Ernie Ford
56	27	22	15	24	O	● Heartbreak Hotel			2:06	Elvis Presley
93	29	26	14	25	O	▲ Dreamlover			3:53	Mariah Carey
93	23	20	14	26	O	▲ That's The Way Love Goes			4:27	Janet Jackson
83	22	20	13	27	O	● Every Breath You Take			4:13	The Police
92	21	18	13	28	O	▲² Jump			3:12	Kris Kross
78	20	18	13	29	O	▲ Night Fever			3:32	Bee Gees
96	20	16	12	30	O	▲² Tha Crossroads			3:48	Bone thugs-n-harmony
76	23	17	11	31	O	● Tonight's The Night (Gonna Be Alright)			3:55	Rod Stewart
						Pos 1 7 Wks				
95	34	28	18	32	O	▲ Waterfalls			4:09	TLC
57	34	24	17	33	O	● Love Letters In The Sand			2:12	Pat Boone
95	30	27	15	34	O	● Take A Bow			5:13	Madonna
93	29	23	15	35	O	▲ Can't Help Falling In Love			3:18	UB40
57	27	19	15	36	O	▲² Jailhouse Rock			2:10	Elvis Presley
95	29	24	14	37	O	▲ This Is How We Do It			3:56	Montell Jordan
57	25	18	14	38	O	▲ (Let Me Be Your) Teddy Bear			1:43	Elvis Presley

YR	WEEKS CH	WEEKS 40	WEEKS 10	RANK	G O L D	PEAK POSITION / PEAK WEEKS	S Y M	TIME	ARTIST
						Pos **1 7** Wks Cont'd			
93	25	19	13	39	O	▲ Informer		4:05	Snow
78	25	19	12	40	O	▲ Shadow Dancing		4:34	Andy Gibb
58	21	18	12	41	O	● At The Hop		2:31	Danny & The Juniors
61	23	17	12	42	O	Tossin' And Turnin'		2:40	Bobby Lewis
82	20	16	12	43	O	▲ I Love Rock 'N Roll		2:45	Joan Jett & The Blackhearts
82	19	15	12	44	O	● Ebony And Ivory		3:41	Paul McCartney/ Stevie Wonder
64	15	14	12	45	O	● I Want To Hold Your Hand		2:24	The Beatles
66	15	13	12	46	O	● I'm A Believer		2:41	The Monkees
83	24	17	11	47	O	▲ Billie Jean		4:50	Michael Jackson
68	15	15	11	48	O	I Heard It Through The Grapevine		2:59	Marvin Gaye
91	22	17	10	49	O	▲³ (Everything I Do) I Do It For You		4:03	Bryan Adams
91	20	15	10	50	O	▲ Black Or White		3:19	Michael Jackson
						Pos **1 6** Wks			
94	41	33	21	51	O	▲ The Sign		3:10	Ace Of Base
96	33	30	19	52	O	▲ Because You Loved Me		4:23	Celine Dion
94	27	25	17	53	O	▲ On Bended Knee		5:25	Boyz II Men
55	21	21	17	54	O	● Love Is A Many-Splendored Thing		2:56	Four Aces
56	25	20	16	55	O	● Rock And Roll Waltz		2:53	Kay Starr
56	24	20	16	56	O	● The Poor People Of Paris .... [I]		2:24	Les Baxter & His Orch.
55	19	19	16	57	O	● The Yellow Rose Of Texas		3:00	Mitch Miller Chorus
78	25	19	15	58	O	▲ Le Freak		3:30	Chic
56	24	19	15	59	O	● Memories Are Made Of This		2:15	Dean Martin
82	25	18	15	60	O	▲² Eye Of The Tiger		3:45	Survivor
83	25	20	14	61	O	● Flashdance...What A Feeling		3:55	Irene Cara
57	26	19	14	62	O	● April Love		2:39	Pat Boone
80	25	19	13	63	O	● Lady		3:51	Kenny Rogers
83	22	18	13	64	O	▲ Say Say Say		3:55	Paul McCartney/ Michael Jackson
59	21	18	13	65	O	● The Battle Of New Orleans		2:33	Johnny Horton
57	21	17	13	66	O	● Young Love		2:24	Tab Hunter
82	25	20	12	67	O	● Centerfold		3:35	The J. Geils Band
80	25	19	12	68	O	● Call Me		3:30	Blondie
58	22	19	12	69	O	● It's All In The Game		2:25	Tommy Edwards
79	22	16	12	70	O	● My Sharona		3:58	The Knack
69	17	16	11	71	O	▲ Aquarius/Let The Sunshine In (The Flesh Failures)		4:45	The 5th Dimension
72	18	15	11	72	O	● The First Time Ever I Saw Your Face		4:15	Roberta Flack
72	18	15	11	73	O	● Alone Again (Naturally)		3:40	Gilbert O'Sullivan
71	17	15	11	74	O	● Joy To The World		3:17	Three Dog Night
60	16	14	11	75	O	▲² Are You Lonesome To-night?		3:07	Elvis Presley
58	14	14	10	76	O	● The Purple People Eater .... [N]		2:11	Sheb Wooley
70	14	13	10	77	O	● Bridge Over Troubled Water		4:55	Simon & Garfunkel
84	19	14	9	78	O	● Like A Virgin		3:35	Madonna
69	13	12	9	79	O	● In The Year 2525 (Exordium & Terminus)		3:15	Zager & Evans
						Pos **1 5** Wks			
57	31	23	16	80	O	● Tammy		3:00	Debbie Reynolds
55	20	20	16	81	O	● The Ballad Of Davy Crockett		2:20	Bill Hayes
92	28	24	15	82	O	▲² Baby Got Back		4:24	Sir Mix-A-Lot
56	23	19	15	83	O	▲² Love Me Tender		2:42	Elvis Presley
56	23	20	14	84	O	● My Prayer		2:45	The Platters
80	22	19	14	85	O	● (Just Like) Starting Over		3:54	John Lennon

YR	WEEKS			RANK	G O L D	PEAK POSITION	PEAK WEEKS	S Y M	TIME	ARTIST
	CH	40	10							

Pos **1** **5** Wks Cont'd

YR	CH	40	10	RANK	GOLD	PEAK POSITION		SYM	TIME	ARTIST
93	22	18	14	86	O ▲	I'd Do Anything For Love (But I Won't Do That)			5:08	Meat Loaf
92	27	23	13	87	O ●	Save The Best For Last			3:39	Vanessa Williams
95	24	20	12	88	O	Have You Ever Really Loved A Woman?			4:45	Bryan Adams
77	23	17	12	89	O ●	Best Of My Love			3:40	Emotions
58	19	16	12	90	O ●	All I Have To Do Is Dream			2:17	The Everly Brothers
84	21	16	11	91	O ▲	When Doves Cry			3:49	Prince
60	20	16	11	92	O ▲	It's Now Or Never			3:12	Elvis Presley
58	19	16	11	93	O ●	Tequila	[I]		2:09	The Champs
70	16	16	11	94	O	I'll Be There			3:35	The Jackson 5
76	19	15	11	95	O ●	Silly Love Songs			5:54	Wings
71	17	15	11	96	O ●	Maggie May			5:15	Rod Stewart
62	18	14	11	97	O ●	I Can't Stop Loving You			2:37	Ray Charles
58	20	16	10	98	O ▲	Don't			2:48	Elvis Presley
84	21	15	10	99	O ●	Jump			4:04	Van Halen
79	20	15	10	100	O ▲	Bad Girls			3:55	Donna Summer
				≀	≀	≀ ≀ ≀ ≀	≀			
68	18	15	10	101	O ●	Love Is Blue	[I]		2:31	Paul Mauriat & His Orch.
71	17	15	10	102	O ●	It's Too Late			3:51	Carole King
59	17	14	10	103	O ●	Venus			2:21	Frankie Avalon
62	16	14	10	104	O ●	Big Girls Don't Cry			2:25	The 4 Seasons
58	16	13	10	105	O ●	Nel Blu Dipinto Di Blu (Volare)	[F]		3:29	Domenico Modugno
61	16	13	10	106	O ●	Big Bad John	[S]		2:57	Jimmy Dean
63	15	13	10	107	O ●	Sugar Shack			2:01	Jimmy Gilmer & The Fireballs
68	15	13	10	108	O ●	Honey			3:58	Bobby Goldsboro
91	19	15	9	109	O ●	Rush, Rush			4:14	Paula Abdul
67	17	15	9	110	O ●	To Sir With Love			2:44	Lulu
60	17	13	9	111	O ●	Cathy's Clown			2:22	The Everly Brothers
73	16	13	9	112	O ●	Killing Me Softly With His Song			4:46	Roberta Flack
68	14	13	9	113	O ●	People Got To Be Free			2:57	The Rascals
71	15	12	9	114	O ●	One Bad Apple			2:45	The Osmonds
69	12	12	9	115	O ●	Get Back			3:08	The Beatles with Billy Preston
66	13	11	9	116	O ●	The Ballad Of The Green Berets			2:27	SSgt Barry Sadler
62	14	12	7	117	O ●	Sherry			2:07	The 4 Seasons
64	10	9	6	118	O ●	Can't Buy Me Love			2:12	The Beatles

Pos **1** **4** Wks

YR	CH	40	10	RANK	GOLD	PEAK POSITION		SYM	TIME	ARTIST
95	32	29	20	119	O ▲	Creep			4:21	TLC
55	26	26	18	120	O ●	Autumn Leaves	[I]		2:52	Roger Williams
56	29	24	17	121	O ●	Lisbon Antigua	[I]		2:33	Nelson Riddle & His Orch.
94	33	26	16	122	O ▲	The Power Of Love			4:46	Celine Dion
93	30	25	16	123	O ▲	Hero			4:17	Mariah Carey
77	31	23	16	124	O ●	I Just Want To Be Your Everything			3:32	Andy Gibb
56	23	19	14	125	O ●	I Almost Lost My Mind			2:27	Pat Boone
80	29	17	14	126	O ●	Upside Down			3:37	Diana Ross
57	28	23	13	127	O ●	Honeycomb			2:14	Jimmie Rodgers
78	27	22	13	128	O ▲	Stayin' Alive			3:41	Bee Gees
70	22	19	13	129	O ●	Raindrops Keep Fallin' On My Head			3:02	B.J. Thomas
83	24	17	13	130	O ●	All Night Long (All Night)			4:16	Lionel Richie
82	23	17	13	131	O ●	Maneater			4:30	Daryl Hall & John Oates
94	25	23	12	132	O ▲	Bump N' Grind			4:07	R. Kelly
57	26	20	12	133	O ●	Wake Up Little Susie			1:57	The Everly Brothers

YR	CH	40	10	RANK	G O L D	PEAK POSITION	PEAK WEEKS	S Y M	TIME	ARTIST
						Pos **1** **4** Wks Cont'd				
80	25	19	12	134	O ●	Another Brick In The Wall (Part II)			3:10	Pink Floyd
58	23	19	12	135	O ●	Sugartime.			2:29	The McGuire Sisters
69	22	18	12	136	O ●	Sugar, Sugar			2:48	The Archies
79	21	18	12	137	O ▲	Da Ya Think I'm Sexy?			5:21	Rod Stewart
78	23	17	12	138	O ●	Kiss You All Over			3:30	Exile
80	22	17	12	139	O ●	Crazy Little Thing Called Love.			2:44	Queen
55	16	16	12	140	O ●	Let Me Go Lover			2:20	Joan Weber
83	29	18	11	141	O ●	Total Eclipse Of The Heart.			4:29	Bonnie Tyler
73	23	17	11	142	O ●	Tie A Yellow Ribbon Round The Ole Oak Tree			3:19	Dawn Feat. Tony Orlando
72	19	17	11	143	O ●	American Pie - Parts I & II			8:36	Don McLean
70	17	15	11	144	O ●	(They Long To Be) Close To You			3:40	Carpenters
68	16	14	11	145	O ●	(Sittin' On) The Dock Of The Bay			2:38	Otis Redding
69	15	14	11	146	O ●	Honky Tonk Women			3:03	The Rolling Stones
83	25	19	10	147	O ●	Down Under.			3:41	Men At Work
86	23	17	10	148	O ●	That's What Friends Are For			3:58	Dionne & Friends
82	22	17	10	149	O ●	Jack & Diane			4:16	John Cougar
90	23	16	10	150	O ●	Because I Love You (The Postman Song)			4:15	Stevie B
79	23	15	10	151	O ▲	Reunited.			3:58	Peaches & Herb
90	21	15	10	152	O ▲	Nothing Compares 2 U			5:09	Sinéad O'Connor
59	21	15	10	153	O ●	Stagger Lee			2:20	Lloyd Price
89	18	14	10	154	O ●	Another Day In Paradise			4:48	Phil Collins
59	17	14	10	155	O ●	The Three Bells			2:47	The Browns
59	15	14	10	156	O ●	Lonely Boy.			2:33	Paul Anka
71	15	14	10	157	O ●	How Can You Mend A Broken Heart . .			3:52	The Bee Gees
60	16	13	10	158	O ▲	Stuck On You			2:17	Elvis Presley
62	15	13	10	159	O ●	Roses Are Red (My Love)			2:37	Bobby Vinton
70	14	13	10	160	O ●	My Sweet Lord			4:39	George Harrison
67	16	12	10	161	O ●	Daydream Believer			2:57	The Monkees
80	24	19	9	162	O ▲	Rock With You			3:20	Michael Jackson
80	23	16	9	163	O ●	Magic			4:25	Olivia Newton-John
85	20	16	9	164	O ●	Say You, Say Me			3:59	Lionel Richie
80	23	15	9	165	O ▲	Funkytown			3:57	Lipps, Inc.
87	20	15	9	166	O ●	Faith			3:14	George Michael
73	18	15	9	167	O ●	My Love			4:07	Paul McCartney & Wings
69	19	14	9	168	O ●	Everyday People			2:18	Sly & The Family Stone
72	19	14	9	169	O ●	Without You			3:16	Nilsson
58	19	14	9	170	O ●	He's Got The Whole World (In His Hands)			2:20	Laurie London
69	15	13	9	171	O ●	Dizzy.			2:55	Tommy Roe
67	14	13	9	172	O ●	Windy			2:49	The Association
67	20	12	9	173	O ●	Ode To Billie Joe			4:13	Bobbie Gentry
61	17	12	9	174	O ●	Runaway.			2:20	Del Shannon
63	15	12	9	175	O	He's So Fine.			1:53	The Chiffons
65	14	12	9	176	O ●	(I Can't Get No) Satisfaction			3:45	The Rolling Stones
63	13	12	9	177	O	Dominique . . . . [F]			2:53	The Singing Nun
64	13	12	9	178	O	There! I've Said It Again			2:20	Bobby Vinton
67	13	11	9	179	O ●	Somethin' Stupid			2:35	Nancy Sinatra & Frank Sinatra
67	13	11	9	180	O ●	Groovin'			2:25	The Young Rascals
86	23	15	8	181	O ●	Walk Like An Egyptian.			3:21	Bangles
76	20	15	8	182	O ●	Don't Go Breaking My Heart			4:23	Elton John & Kiki Dee
72	20	14	8	183	O ●	I Can See Clearly Now			2:48	Johnny Nash
89	20	13	8	184	O ▲	Miss You Much			3:55	Janet Jackson
76	19	13	8	185	O ▲	Disco Lady.			4:20	Johnnie Taylor
67	16	13	8	186	O ●	The Letter.			1:58	The Box Tops
85	18	12	8	187	O	▲⁴ We Are The World.			6:22	USA for Africa

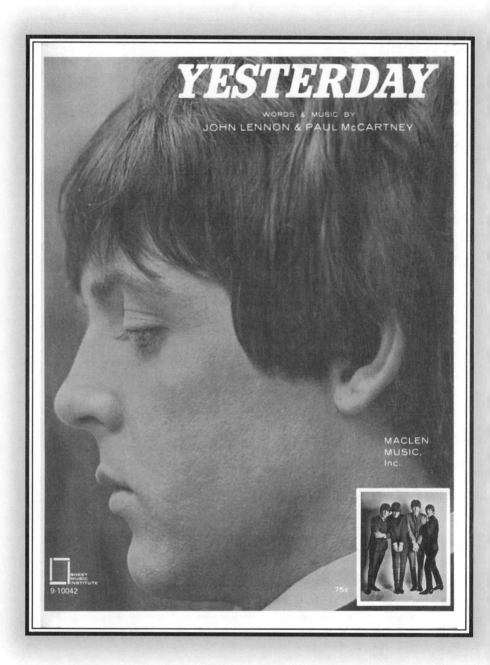

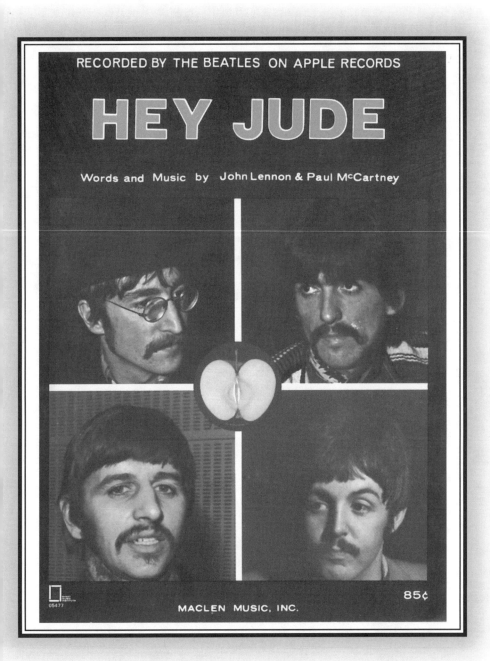

YR	WEEKS			RANK	G O L D	PEAK POSITION	PEAK WEEKS	S Y M	TIME	ARTIST
	CH	40	10							

Pos 1 — 4 Wks Cont'd

YR	CH	40	10	RANK	GOLD	PEAK		SYM	TIME	ARTIST
59	16	12	8	188	O	● Come Softly To Me			2:25	Fleetwoods
68	14	12	8	189	O	● This Guy's In Love With You			3:55	Herb Alpert
64	13	12	8	190	O	● Baby Love			2:34	The Supremes
90	22	17	7	191	O	● Vision Of Love			3:22	Mariah Carey
88	18	14	7	192	O	Roll With It			4:30	Steve Winwood
87	21	13	7	193	O	Livin' On A Prayer			4:12	Bon Jovi
75	23	16	6	194	O	● Love Will Keep Us Together			3:15	The Captain & Tennille
58	28	13	6	195	O	● The Chipmunk Song [X-N]			2:17	The Chipmunks/David Seville
65	11	9	6	196	O	● Yesterday			2:04	The Beatles

Pos 1 — 3 Wks

YR	CH	40	10	RANK	GOLD	PEAK		SYM	TIME	ARTIST
60	39	33	25	197	O	● The Twist			2:32	Chubby Checker
95	38	36	22	198	O	▲³ Gangsta's Paradise			4:00	Coolio Featuring L.V.
56	26	22	18	199	O	● The Green Door			2:11	Jim Lowe
77	33	26	17	200	O	● How Deep Is Your Love			3:30	Bee Gees
94	30	25	16	201	O	● Stay (I Missed You)			3:00	Lisa Loeb & Nine Stories
55	20	20	16	202	O	● Dance With Me Henry (Wallflower)			2:15	Georgia Gibbs
56	27	22	15	203	O	● Moonglow and Theme From "Picnic" [I]			2:47	Morris Stoloff & His Orch.
80	31	21	15	204	O	▲ Another One Bites The Dust			3:32	Queen
94	22	20	14	205	O	▲ All For Love			4:39	Bryan Adams/Rod Stewart/Sting
55	20	20	14	206	O	● Hearts Of Stone			2:03	The Fontane Sisters
79	21	17▶	14	207	O	▲ Hot Stuff			3:47	Donna Summer
77	25	18	13	208	O	● Love Theme From "A Star Is Born" (Evergreen)			3:03	Barbra Streisand
79	27	17	13	209	O	▲ I Will Survive			3:15	Gloria Gaynor
57	26	17	13	210	O	● You Send Me			2:41	Sam Cooke
82	28	21	12	211	O	● Don't You Want Me			3:56	The Human League
58	19	18	12	212	O	● Witch Doctor [N]			2:15	David Seville
81	24	17	12	213	O	● Arthur's Theme (Best That You Can Do)			3:53	Christopher Cross
78	23	17	12	214	O	▲ Boogie Oogie Oogie			3:45	A Taste Of Honey
92	21	17	12	215	O	▲ I'm Too Sexy [N]			2:50	Right Said Fred
80	24	19	11	216	O	● Woman In Love			3:48	Barbra Streisand
60	23	18	11	217	O	● I'm Sorry			2:40	Brenda Lee
58	23	18	11	218	O	● To Know Him, Is To Love Him			2:18	The Teddy Bears
84	23	16	11	219	O	▲ Footloose			3:46	Kenny Loggins
80	21	16	11	220	O	● Coming Up (Live at Glasgow)			3:54	Paul McCartney & Wings
70	19	16	11	221	O	● I Think I Love You			2:50	The Partridge Family
71	18	16	11	222	O	● Knock Three Times			2:56	Dawn
62	18	14	11	223	O	● Peppermint Twist - Part I			2:00	Joey Dee & the Starliters
73	17	14	11	224	O	● You're So Vain			4:25	Carly Simon
84	28	18	10	225	O	● What's Love Got To Do With It			3:49	Tina Turner
83	25	18	10	226	O	▲ Beat It			4:11	Michael Jackson
76	25	18	10	227	O	▲ Play That Funky Music			3:12	Wild Cherry
78	32	16	10	228	O	● Baby Come Back			3:28	Player
84	24	16	10	229	O	● Against All Odds (Take A Look At Me Now)			3:24	Phil Collins
79	21	16	10	230	O	● Escape (The Pina Colada Song)			3:50	Rupert Holmes
59	19	16	10	231	O	● Smoke Gets In Your Eyes			2:39	The Platters
84	26	15	10	232	O	● I Just Called To Say I Love You			4:16	Stevie Wonder
61	17	15	10	233	O	● Wonderland By Night [I]			3:12	Bert Kaempfert & His Orch.

YR	CH	40	10	RANK	GOLD	PEAK POSITION	PEAK WEEKS	SYM	TIME	ARTIST

Pos **1**³ Wks Cont'd

YR	CH	40	10	RANK	GOLD	Title	SYM	TIME	ARTIST
60	27	14	10	234	O ●	Running Bear		2:33	Johnny Preston
84	21	14	10	235	O ●	Ghostbusters		3:46	Ray Parker Jr.
57	20	14	10	236	O	Butterfly		2:17	Andy Williams
71	18	14	10	237	O ●	Brand New Key		2:26	Melanie
66	15	13	10	238	O ●	Winchester Cathedral		2:23	New Vaudeville Band
72	14	12	10	239	O ●	A Horse With No Name		4:10	America
92	24	17	9	240	O ●	To Be With You		3:20	Mr. Big
74	23	17	9	241	O ●	The Way We Were		3:29	Barbra Streisand
85	21	17	9	242	O ▲	Careless Whisper		4:50	Wham!/George Michael
84	22	16	9	243	O ●	Karma Chameleon		4:05	Culture Club
78	20	15	9	244	O ●	MacArthur Park		3:59	Donna Summer
67	23	14	9	245	O ●	Light My Fire		2:52	The Doors
60	18	14	9	246	O ●	Save The Last Dance For Me		2:34	The Drifters
73	17	14	9	247	O ▲	Crocodile Rock		3:56	Elton John
57	17	14	9	248	O ▲	Too Much		2:30	Elvis Presley
72	18	13	9	249	O ●	Baby Don't Get Hooked On Me		3:02	Mac Davis
71	15	13	9	250	O ●	Go Away Little Girl		2:30	Donny Osmond
71	14	13	9	251	O ●	Family Affair		3:04	Sly & The Family Stone
70	14	13	9	252	O	Ain't No Mountain High Enough		3:28	Diana Ross
67	15	12	9	253	O ●	Happy Together		2:50	The Turtles
63	15	12	9	254	O ●	Hey Paula		2:25	Paul & Paula
63	14	12	9	255	O	My Boyfriend's Back		2:11	The Angels
81	23	17	8	256	O ●	Kiss On My List		3:48	Daryl Hall & John Oates
90	24	16	8	257	O ▲²	Vogue		4:19	Madonna
74	21	15	8	258	O	Seasons In The Sun		3:24	Terry Jacks
87	21	15	8	259	O	Alone		3:38	Heart
84	24	14	8	260	O ▲	Wake Me Up Before You Go-Go		3:51	Wham!
88	21	14	8	261	O ●	Every Rose Has Its Thorn		4:20	Poison
85	18	14	8	262	O ●	Can't Fight This Feeling		4:54	REO Speedwagon
90	17	14	8	263	O ●	Escapade		4:41	Janet Jackson
61	16	14	8	264	O	Pony Time		2:27	Chubby Checker
72	16	14	8	265	O ●	Me And Mrs. Jones		4:42	Billy Paul
64	15	14	8	266	O ●	Oh, Pretty Woman		2:55	Roy Orbison
70	15	14	8	267	O ●	American Woman		3:51	The Guess Who
69	15	14	8	268	O ▲	Wedding Bell Blues		2:42	The 5th Dimension
85	22	13	8	269	O	Money For Nothing		4:38	Dire Straits
88	18	13	8	270	O	With Or Without You		4:56	U2
77	17	13	8	271	O	Sir Duke		3:53	Stevie Wonder
62	16	13	8	272	O	Telstar [I]		3:14	The Tornadoes
70	15	13	8	273	O	War		3:12	Edwin Starr
61	15	13	8	274	●	The Lion Sleeps Tonight		2:35	The Tokens
62	14	13	8	275	O	Soldier Boy		2:40	The Shirelles
74	17	12	8	276	O ●	The Streak [N]		3:15	Ray Stevens
63	15	12	8	277	O ●	Blue Velvet		2:46	Bobby Vinton
62	15	12	8	278	O ●	Hey! Baby		2:23	Bruce Channel
63	14	12	8	279	O ●	Sukiyaki [F]		3:05	Kyu Sakamoto
62	15	11	8	280	O ●	Duke Of Earl		2:22	Gene Chandler
65	14	11	8	281	O	Turn! Turn! Turn! (To Everything There Is A Season)		3:34	The Byrds
61	14	11	8	282	O	Blue Moon		2:15	The Marcels
63	14	11	8	283	O	I Will Follow Him		2:25	Little Peggy March
66	13	11	8	284	O ●	(You're My) Soul And Inspiration		3:00	The Righteous Brothers
66	12	10	8	285	O ●	Monday, Monday		3:09	The Mama's & The Papa's
67	11	10	8	286	O ●	Hello Goodbye		3:24	The Beatles
64	11	10	8	287	O	The House Of The Rising Sun		2:58	The Animals
91	20	20	7	288	O ●	Emotions		4:09	Mariah Carey

YR	WEEKS			RANK	G O L D		PEAK POSITION	PEAK WEEKS	S Y M	TIME	ARTIST
	CH	40	10								

Pos 1 3 Wks Cont'd

YR	CH	40	10	RANK	GOLD		TITLE		SYM	TIME	ARTIST
90	26	18	7	289	O	●	Love Takes Time			3:40	Mariah Carey
89	25	16	7	290	O	▲	Straight Up			4:11	Paula Abdul
72	21	16	7	291	O	●	The Candy Man			3:10	Sammy Davis, Jr.
82	23	15	7	292	O	▲	Up Where We Belong			4:00	Joe Cocker & Jennifer Warnes
86	23	15	7	293	O	●	On My Own			4:30	Patti LaBelle/ Michael McDonald
90	23	14	7	294	O	●	Opposites Attract			3:45	Paula Abdul with The Wild Pair
87	21	14	7	295	O		La Bamba	[F]		2:54	Los Lobos
72	19	14	7	296	O	●	Lean On Me			3:45	Bill Withers
86	18	14	7	297	O	●	Greatest Love Of All			4:30	Whitney Houston
88	18	14	7	298	O	●	One More Try			5:50	George Michael
89	21	13	7	299	O	▲	Right Here Waiting			4:21	Richard Marx
85	19	13	7	300	O	●	Shout			3:59	Tears For Fears
86	19	13	7	301	O		Stuck With You			4:20	Huey Lewis & the News
75	17	13	7	302	O	●	Fly, Robin, Fly	[I]		3:05	Silver Convention
86	17	13	7	303	O		Rock Me Amadeus			3:10	Falco
89	19	12	7	304	O	●	Lost In Your Eyes			3:34	Debbie Gibson
89	16	12	7	305	O	▲	Like A Prayer			5:19	Madonna
75	15	12	7	306	O	▲	Island Girl			3:46	Elton John
63	15	12	7	307	O		Fingertips - Pt 2			2:49	Little Stevie Wonder
68	13	12	7	308	O	●	Mrs. Robinson			4:00	Simon & Garfunkel
63	13	12	7	309	O		Walk Like A Man			2:11	The 4 Seasons
61	15	11	7	310	O	●	Take Good Care Of My Baby			2:27	Bobby Vee
90	15	11	7	311	O	▲	Step By Step			4:18	New Kids On The Block
64	13	11	7	312	O		Chapel Of Love			2:45	The Dixie Cups
66	12	11	7	313	O		We Can Work It Out			2:10	The Beatles
65	11	11	7	314	O		Mrs. Brown You've Got A Lovely Daughter			2:46	Herman's Hermits
64	11	11	7	315	O	●	I Feel Fine			2:20	The Beatles
65	14	10	7	316	O	●	I Got You Babe			3:09	Sonny & Cher
66	11	10	7	317	O	●	Summer In The City			2:39	The Lovin' Spoonful
90	23	16	6	318	O		How Am I Supposed To Live Without You			4:14	Michael Bolton
76	27	15	6	319	O	●	December, 1963 (Oh, What a Night)			3:21	The Four Seasons
76	17	13	6	320	O	●	50 Ways To Leave Your Lover			3:29	Paul Simon
66	14	12	6	321	O	●	Cherish			3:00	The Association
65	13	12	6	322	O	●	Help!			2:16	The Beatles
74	15	11	6	323	O	●	(You're) Having My Baby			2:32	Paul Anka with Odia Coates
75	14	10	6	324	O	●	He Don't Love You (Like I Love You)			3:36	Tony Orlando & Dawn
75	14	12	5	325	O	●	Bad Blood			3:06	Neil Sedaka

Pos 1 2 Wks

YR	CH	40	10	RANK	GOLD		TITLE		SYM	TIME	ARTIST
55	21	21	18	326	O		Unchained Melody			2:30	Les Baxter Chorus
55	21	21	18	327	O		Learnin' The Blues			2:59	Frank Sinatra
93	24	22	16	328	O	▲	Freak Me			4:28	Silk
96	32	26	15	329	O	▲	Always Be My Baby			4:16	Mariah Carey
94	30	23	15	330	O	▲	Here Comes The Hotstepper			4:04	Ini Kamoze
93	26	22	15	331	O	▲	Weak			4:16	SWV (Sisters With Voices)

YR	WEEKS			RANK	G O L D	PEAK POSITION	PEAK WEEKS	S Y M	TIME	ARTIST
	CH	40	10							
						Pos **1 2** Wks Cont'd				
93	23	22	15	332	O	▲ Again			3:47	Janet Jackson
55	20	20	15	333	O	● Ain't That A Shame			2:22	Pat Boone
57	29	19	14	334	O	● Round And Round			2:30	Perry Como
82	25	19	14	335	O	● Abracadabra			3:34	The Steve Miller Band
56	24	19	14	336	O	● The Great Pretender			2:38	The Platters
73	19	17	13	337	O	Let's Get It On			3:58	Marvin Gaye
81	32	22	12	338	O	● Jessie's Girl			3:14	Rick Springfield
83	25	18	12	339	O	▲ Islands In The Stream			4:08	Kenny Rogers with Dolly Parton
82	24	18	12	340	O	● Hard To Say I'm Sorry			3:42	Chicago
78	29	22	11	341	O	● (Love Is) Thicker Than Water			3:18	Andy Gibb
96	24	21	11	342	O	▲² How Do U Want It			4:00	2 Pac (featuring KC & JoJo)
80	21	19	11	343	O	● It's Still Rock And Roll To Me			2:55	Billy Joel
78	20	16	11	344	O	Three Times A Lady			3:35	Commodores
79	21	15	11	345	O	Ring My Bell			3:30	Anita Ward
69	17	15	11	346	O	I Can't Get Next To You			2:53	The Temptations
68	16	15	11	347	O	Love Child			2:59	Diana Ross & The Supremes
69	16	15	11	348	O	Crimson And Clover			3:23	Tommy James & The Shondells
58	15	15	11	349	O	● Poor Little Fool			2:29	Ricky Nelson
79	19	14	11	350	O	● Babe			4:26	Styx
64	15	14	11	351	O	She Loves You			2:18	The Beatles
70	14	13	11	352	O	● Let It Be			3:50	The Beatles
84	24	17	10	353	O	● Hello			4:07	Lionel Richie
84	23	17	10	354	O	Owner Of A Lonely Heart			3:50	Yes
58	21	17	10	355	O	● It's Only Make Believe			2:10	Conway Twitty
77	22	16	10	356	O	● Torn Between Two Lovers			3:40	Mary MacGregor
59	20	16	10	357	O	Heartaches By The Number			2:39	Guy Mitchell
92	20	16	10	358	O	● How Do You Talk To An Angel			3:40	The Heights
73	19	16	10	359	O	Keep On Truckin' (Part 1)			3:33	Eddie Kendricks
78	17	15	10	360	O	● You Don't Bring Me Flowers			3:14	Barbra & Neil
60	18	14	10	361	O	● Teen Angel			2:38	Mark Dinning
60	17	14	10	362	O	My Heart Has A Mind Of Its Own			2:25	Connie Francis
70	16	14	10	363	O	The Tears Of A Clown			2:56	Smokey Robinson & The Miracles
82	18	13	10	364	O	● Truly			3:19	Lionel Richie
65	14	13	10	365	O	I Can't Help Myself			2:43	Four Tops
83	32	18	9	366	O	● Baby, Come To Me			3:30	Patti Austin with James Ingram
81	28	18	9	367	O	● I Love A Rainy Night			3:08	Eddie Rabbitt
81	26	18	9	368	O	● 9 To 5			2:42	Dolly Parton
75	23	18	9	369	O	● Rhinestone Cowboy			3:08	Glen Campbell
76	26	17	9	370	O	▲ Kiss And Say Goodbye			3:29	Manhattans
91	25	17	9	371	O	▲ Gonna Make You Sweat (Everybody Dance Now)			4:03	C & C Music Factory
90	25	17	9	372	O	● It Must Have Been Love			3:43	Roxette
81	23	17	9	373	O	● Private Eyes			3:29	Daryl Hall & John Oates
75	21	17	9	374	O	▲ Philadelphia Freedom			5:38	The Elton John Band
76	21	17	9	375	O	● If You Leave Me Now			3:53	Chicago
79	21	17	9	376	O	▲ Too Much Heaven			4:54	Bee Gees
84	23	16	9	377	O	Out Of Touch			3:55	Daryl Hall/John Oates
83	22	16	9	378	O	Maniac			4:13	Michael Sembello
60	22	16	9	379	O	El Paso			4:40	Marty Robbins
79	25	15	9	380	O	● Rise		[I]	3:47	Herb Alpert
85	22	15	9	381	O	Broken Wings			4:29	Mr. Mister

17

YR	WEEKS			RANK	G O L D	PEAK POSITION	PEAK WEEKS	S Y M	TIME	ARTIST
	CH	40	10							

Pos 1 ² Wks Cont'd

YR	CH	40	10	RANK	GOLD	PEAK POSITION	SYM	TIME	ARTIST
84	20	14	9	382	O ●	Time After Time		3:59	Cyndi Lauper
84	19	14	9	383	O ▲	Let's Hear It For The Boy		4:20	Deniece Williams
84	19	14	9	384	O ●	Let's Go Crazy		3:46	Prince & the Revolution
87	18	14	9	385	O ▲	I Wanna Dance With Somebody (Who Loves Me)		4:36	Whitney Houston
71	16	14	9	386	O ●	Gypsys, Tramps & Thieves		2:36	Cher
79	20	13	9	387	O ▲	Tragedy		5:00	Bee Gees
76	18	13	9	388	O	Love Hangover		3:40	Diana Ross
59	18	13	9	389	O ●	Sleep Walk	[I]	2:20	Santo & Johnny
61	17	13	9	390	O ●	Calcutta	[I]	2:13	Lawrence Welk & His Orch.
65	16	13	9	391	O	You've Lost That Lovin' Feelin'		3:47	The Righteous Brothers
75	16	13	9	392	O	That's The Way (I Like It)		3:06	KC & The Sunshine Band
64	15	13	9	393	O ●	I Get Around		2:12	The Beach Boys
71	15	13	9	394	O	Just My Imagination (Running Away With Me)		3:39	The Temptations
65	15	13	9	395	O ●	Downtown		2:58	Petula Clark
62	15	13	9	396	O	Johnny Angel		2:16	Shelley Fabares
70	15	13	9	397	O ●	Mama Told Me (Not To Come)		2:58	Three Dog Night
68	15	13	9	398	O ●	Tighten Up		2:38	Archie Bell & The Drells
79	15	13	9	399	O ●	No More Tears (Enough Is Enough)		4:39	Barbra Streisand/ Donna Summer
64	14	13	9	400	O	Come See About Me		2:39	The Supremes
64	14	13	9	401	O	Where Did Our Love Go		2:32	The Supremes
63	17	12	9	402	O ●	Go Away Little Girl		2:07	Steve Lawrence
61	14	12	9	403	O ●	Runaround Sue		2:40	Dion
70	13	12	9	404	O	ABC		2:38	The Jackson 5
70	13	12	9	405	O	The Love You Save		2:42	The Jackson 5
71	13	12	9	406	O ●	Theme From Shaft		3:15	Isaac Hayes
64	13	12	9	407	O	Do Wah Diddy Diddy		2:19	Manfred Mann
61	17	11	9	408	O ●	Michael		2:45	The Highwaymen
65	12	11	9	409	O ●	This Diamond Ring		2:05	Gary Lewis & The Playboys
68	12	11	9	410	O ●	Hello, I Love You		2:13	The Doors
62	37	24	8	411	O ●	Monster Mash	[N]	3:01	Bobby "Boris" Pickett
91	25	18	8	412	O ●	The First Time		4:15	Surface
88	24	16	8	413	O ●	Look Away		3:59	Chicago
73	22	16	8	414	O ●	Bad, Bad Leroy Brown		3:02	Jim Croce
85	21	16	8	415	O ●	I Want To Know What Love Is		4:58	Foreigner
73	20	16	8	416	O ●	Top Of The World		2:56	Carpenters
73	19	16	8	417	O ●	Midnight Train To Georgia		3:55	Gladys Knight & The Pips
60	18	16	8	418	O ●	Everybody's Somebody's Fool		2:40	Connie Francis
78	22	15	8	419	O ▲	Grease		3:21	Frankie Valli
87	22	15	8	420	O ●	Nothing's Gonna Stop Us Now		4:29	Starship
84	21	15	8	421	O ●	The Reflex		4:25	Duran Duran
85	19	15	8	422	O ●	The Power Of Love		3:53	Huey Lewis & The News
89	19	15	8	423	O ●	We Didn't Start The Fire		4:29	Billy Joel
73	18	15	8	424	O ●	Brother Louie		3:55	Stories
61	16	15	8	425	O ●	Travelin' Man		2:12	Ricky Nelson
85	24	14	8	426	O	Everybody Wants To Rule The World		4:10	Tears For Fears
73	22	14	8	427	O ●	Will It Go Round In Circles		3:42	Billy Preston
73	20	14	8	428	O ●	Half-Breed		2:42	Cher
92	20	14	8	429	O	I'll Be There		4:12	Mariah Carey

YR	CH	40	10	RANK	GOLD		PEAK POSITION / PEAK WEEKS / SYM	TIME	ARTIST

Pos **1** **2** Wks Cont'd

YR	CH	40	10	RANK	GOLD	SYM	Title	TIME	ARTIST
81	20	14	8	430	O	●	Rapture	6:33	Blondie
76	20	14	8	431	O	●	Afternoon Delight	3:12	Starland Vocal Band
91	19	14	8	432	O	●	I Don't Wanna Cry	4:49	Mariah Carey
57	17	14	8	433	O	●	Butterfly	2:21	Charlie Gracie
69	16	13	8	434	O	●	Na Na Hey Hey Kiss Him Goodbye	3:45	Steam
68	16	13	8	435	O	●	Judy In Disguise (With Glasses)	2:47	John Fred & His Playboy Band
91	16	13	8	436	O	▲	Justify My Love	4:50	Madonna
64	15	13	8	437	O		My Guy	2:45	Mary Wells
58	15	13	8	438	O	●	Get A Job	2:25	The Silhouettes
78	18	12	8	439	O		With A Little Luck	5:45	Wings
74	18	12	8	440	O	●	Kung Fu Fighting	3:18	Carl Douglas
75	17	12	8	441	O		Jive Talkin'	3:33	Bee Gees
59	16	12	8	442	O	●	Kansas City	2:21	Wilbert Harrison
71	15	12	8	443	O		Me And Bobby McGee	4:09	Janis Joplin
61	15	12	8	444	O	●	Quarter To Three	2:29	U.S. Bonds
69	14	12	8	445	O	●	Love Theme From Romeo & Juliet . . [I]	2:29	Henry Mancini & His Orch.
64	13	12	8	446	O	●	A Hard Day's Night	2:28	The Beatles
71	12	12	8	447	O		Brown Sugar	3:50	The Rolling Stones
61	13	11	8	448	O		Hit The Road Jack	2:00	Ray Charles
66	13	11	8	449	O		You Can't Hurry Love	2:49	The Supremes
61	12	11	8	450	O	▲	Surrender	1:51	Elvis Presley
65	12	10	8	451	O		Stop! In The Name Of Love	2:51	The Supremes
66	11	9	8	452	O		Wild Thing	2:30	The Troggs
81	30	21	7	453	O	▲	Celebration	3:42	Kool & The Gang
91	21	16	7	454	O		Baby Baby	3:44	Amy Grant
91	20	16	7	455	O	●	Cream	4:08	Prince & The N.P.G.
84	26	15	7	456	O	●	Caribbean Queen (No More Love On The Run)	3:32	Billy Ocean
85	24	15	7	457	O	●	We Built This City	4:49	Starship
90	24	15	7	458	O	●	Black Velvet	4:45	Alannah Myles
91	23	15	7	459	O	●	All The Man That I Need	3:43	Whitney Houston
90	22	15	7	460	O	●	Release Me	3:40	Wilson Phillips
61	19	15	7	461	O		Will You Love Me Tomorrow	2:48	The Shirelles
91	19	15	7	462	O	●	Someday	3:55	Mariah Carey
88	24	14	7	463	O	●	Never Gonna Give You Up	3:31	Rick Astley
88	24	14	7	464	O	●	Sweet Child O' Mine	5:55	Guns N' Roses
88	23	14	7	465	O	●	Anything For You	4:02	Gloria Estefan
85	22	14	7	466	O		St. Elmo's Fire (Man In Motion)	4:08	John Parr
91	20	14	7	467	O	●	I Adore Mi Amor	4:45	Color Me Badd
73	20	14	7	468	O	●	The Night The Lights Went Out In Georgia	3:36	Vicki Lawrence
88	20	14	7	469	O		Get Outta My Dreams, Get Into My Car	4:43	Billy Ocean
91	19	14	7	470	O		Coming Out Of The Dark	3:55	Gloria Estefan
90	18	14	7	471	O	●	She Ain't Worth It	3:31	Glenn Medeiros/ Bobby Brown
86	20	13	7	472	O		Kyrie	4:10	Mr. Mister
86	18	13	7	473	O	●	Kiss	3:46	Prince & The Revolution
86	18	13	7	474	O		Papa Don't Preach	3:47	Madonna
89	18	13	7	475	O		Two Hearts	3:23	Phil Collins
87	17	13	7	476	O		I Still Haven't Found What I'm Looking For	4:36	U2
88	17	13	7	477	O		Man In The Mirror	4:55	Michael Jackson
87	17	13	7	478	O		Didn't We Almost Have It All	4:56	Whitney Houston
74	19	12	7	479	O	●	Billy, Don't Be A Hero	3:25	Bo Donaldson & The Heywoods
62	18	12	7	480	O		He's A Rebel	2:25	The Crystals

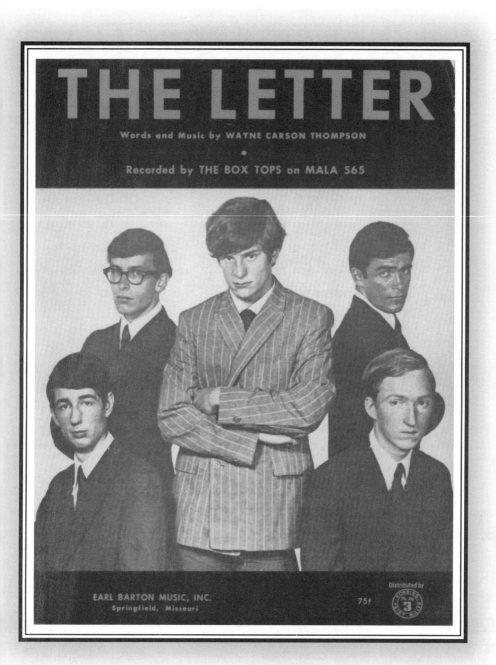

YR	WEEKS			RANK	G O L D	PEAK POSITION	PEAK WEEKS	S Y M	TIME	ARTIST
	CH	40	10							

Pos **1** **2** Wks Cont'd

YR	CH	40	10	RANK	GOLD	TITLE	SYM	TIME	ARTIST
87	17	12	7	481 O		I Knew You Were Waiting (For Me)		3:57	Aretha Franklin & George Michael
73	15	12	7	482 O	●	Time In A Bottle		2:24	Jim Croce
66	15	12	7	483 O		Reach Out I'll Be There		2:58	Four Tops
63	15	12	7	484 O		I'm Leaving It Up To You		2:13	Dale & Grace
62	14	12	7	485 O		Breaking Up Is Hard To Do		2:20	Neil Sedaka
70	13	12	7	486 O	●	Thank You (Falettinme Be Mice Elf Agin)		4:47	Sly & The Family Stone
74	17	11	7	487 O	●	Annie's Song		2:58	John Denver
65	14	11	7	488 O		Help Me, Rhonda		2:45	The Beach Boys
62	13	11	7	489 O	▲	Good Luck Charm		2:23	Elvis Presley
63	13	11	7	490 O		Surf City		2:24	Jan & Dean
63	13	11	7	491 O		It's My Party		2:19	Lesley Gore
63	13	11	7	492 O	●	Walk Right In		2:32	The Rooftop Singers
64	12	11	7	493 O	●	Rag Doll		2:31	The 4 Seasons
67	12	11	7	494 O	●	Respect		2:26	Aretha Franklin
59	14	10	7	495 O	●	A Big Hunk O' Love		2:12	Elvis Presley
63	13	10	7	496 O		Easier Said Than Done		2:08	The Essex
67	13	10	7	497 O		Kind Of A Drag		2:05	The Buckinghams
68	12	10	7	498 O	●	Grazing In The Grass .... [I]		2:25	Hugh Masekela
66	11	10	7	499 O		Paint It, Black		3:19	The Rolling Stones
73	22	17	6	500 O	●	The Most Beautiful Girl		2:42	Charlie Rich
86	23	16	6	501 O	●	How Will I Know		4:10	Whitney Houston
87	24	15	6	502 O	●	At This Moment		4:10	Billy Vera & The Beaters
89	22	15	6	503 O	●	When I See You Smile		4:16	Bad English
81	21	15	6	504 O	●	Morning Train (Nine To Five)		3:20	Sheena Easton
88	27	14	6	505 O		The Flame		4:30	Cheap Trick
89	23	14	6	506 O	▲	Blame It On The Rain		4:06	Milli Vanilli
89	22	14	6	507 O	●	Forever Your Girl		4:12	Paula Abdul
89	22	14	6	508 O	●	Girl I'm Gonna Miss You		4:19	Milli Vanilli
86	21	14	6	509 O		Glory Of Love...................		4:20	Peter Cetera
75	21	14	6	510 O	●	Fame.........................		3:30	David Bowie
74	20	14	6	511 O	●	The Loco-Motion		2:45	Grand Funk
88	20	14	6	512 O	●	Could've Been		3:31	Tiffany
85	20	14	6	513 O	●	Everything She Wants		5:10	Wham!
77	20	14	6	514 O	●	Rich Girl......................		2:23	Daryl Hall & John Oates
85	19	14	6	515 O	●	Heaven		4:03	Bryan Adams
74	18	14	6	516 O	●	TSOP (The Sound Of Philadelphia) .. [I]		3:29	MFSB with The Three Degrees
58	16	14	6	517 O	▲	Hard Headed Woman		1:52	Elvis Presley
88	26	13	6	518 O	●	Don't Worry Be Happy		3:45	Bobby McFerrin
88	25	13	6	519 O	●	Groovy Kind Of Love.............		3:28	Phil Collins
87	24	13	6	520 O		I Think We're Alone Now		3:47	Tiffany
89	20	13	6	521 O	●	Toy Soldiers		4:52	Martika
77	20	13	6	522 O	▲	Star Wars Theme/Cantina Band .... [I]		3:28	Meco
86	19	13	6	523 O	●	When I Think Of You.............		3:56	Janet Jackson
87	19	13	6	524 O		(I Just) Died In Your Arms		4:38	Cutting Crew
88	18	13	6	525 O		Where Do Broken Hearts Go........		4:37	Whitney Houston
85	17	13	6	526 O		A View To A Kill		3:33	Duran Duran
88	17	13	6	527 O		Father Figure		5:37	George Michael
70	15	13	6	528 O	●	Everything Is Beautiful		3:29	Ray Stevens
88	20	12	6	529 O		Bad Medicine		3:52	Bon Jovi
86	20	12	6	530 O		True Colors		3:45	Cyndi Lauper
85	18	12	6	531 O	●	One More Night		4:25	Phil Collins
86	18	12	6	532 O		Amanda		4:16	Boston

YR	WEEKS			RANK	G O L D	PEAK POSITION	PEAK WEEKS	S Y M	TIME	ARTIST
	CH	40	10							

Pos 1 2 Wks Cont'd

YR	CH	40	10	RANK	GOLD	TITLE	SYM	TIME	ARTIST
74	18	12	6	533	O ●	I Can Help		2:57	Billy Swan
87	17	12	6	534	O ●	Lean On Me		3:58	Club Nouveau
72	17	12	6	535	O ●	My Ding-A-Ling [N]		4:18	Chuck Berry
88	16	12	6	536	O	Monkey		4:45	George Michael
73	15	11	6	537	O ●	The Morning After		2:14	Maureen McGovern
62	14	11	6	538	O ●	Sheila		2:02	Tommy Roe
63	14	11	6	539	O	If You Wanna Be Happy		2:14	Jimmy Soul
65	12	11	6	540	O	Get Off Of My Cloud		2:58	The Rolling Stones
75	14	10	6	541	O ●	Lucy In The Sky With Diamonds		5:58	Elton John
66	13	10	6	542	O ●	When A Man Loves A Woman		2:55	Percy Sledge
66	12	10	6	543	O	You Keep Me Hangin' On		2:45	The Supremes
66	12	10	6	544	O ●	Hanky Panky		2:59	Tommy James & The Shondells
70	10	10	6	545	O	The Long And Winding Road		3:40	The Beatles
65	10	10	6	546	O	I Hear A Symphony		2:41	The Supremes
66	13	9	6	547	O	My Love		2:50	Petula Clark
65	11	8	6	548	O	I'm Telling You Now		2:05	Freddie & The Dreamers
66	14	12	5	549	O ●	The Sounds Of Silence		3:05	Simon & Garfunkel
87	14	11	5	550	O	Bad		4:05	Michael Jackson
74	24	10	5	551	O ●	I Honestly Love You		3:36	Olivia Newton-John
74	17	10	5	552	O	Rock Your Baby		3:14	George McCrae
66	10	10	5	553	O ●	Paperback Writer		2:25	The Beatles
65	10	9	5	554	O ●	Eight Days A Week		2:43	The Beatles

Pos 1 1 Wks

YR	CH	40	10	RANK	GOLD	TITLE	SYM	TIME	ARTIST
96	41	39	20	555	O ▲	You're Makin' Me High		4:07	Toni Braxton
95	36	32	17	556	O ●	Kiss From A Rose		4:43	Seal
95	21	20	15	557	O ▲	Exhale (Shoop Shoop)		3:22	Whitney Houston
58	21	17	15	558	O ●	Patricia [I]		2:28	Perez Prado & His Orch.
92	28	25	14	559	O ●	All 4 Love		3:30	Color Me Badd
80	27	22	14	560	O ●	Do That To Me One More Time		3:45	The Captain & Tennille
56	23	20	14	561	O ●	Hot Diggity (Dog Ziggity Boom)		2:19	Perry Como
57	28	22	13	562	O ●	Chances Are		3:00	Johnny Mathis
56	24	19	13	563	O ▲	I Want You, I Need You, I Love You		2:37	Elvis Presley
64	22	19	13	564	O	Hello, Dolly!		2:22	Louis Armstrong
57	22	19	13	565	O ●	Don't Forbid Me		2:14	Pat Boone
57	21	17	13	566	O ●	Young Love		2:29	Sonny James
79	20	15	13	567	O	Still		3:43	Commodores
57	29	18	12	568	O ●	Diana		2:29	Paul Anka
58	21	18	12	569	O ●	Tom Dooley		3:01	The Kingston Trio
82	21	17	12	570	O ●	I Can't Go For That (No Can Do)		3:50	Daryl Hall & John Oates
58	23	16	12	571	O ●	Catch A Falling Star		2:25	Perry Como
58	17	14	12	572	O ●	Twilight Time		2:47	The Platters
80	26	18	11	573	O	Please Don't Go		3:43	K.C. & The Sunshine Band
59	20	17	11	574	O ●	Mr. Blue		2:18	The Fleetwoods
76	21	16	11	575	O	(Shake, Shake, Shake) Shake Your Booty		3:06	KC & The Sunshine Band
58	19	16	11	576	O ●	Little Star		2:37	The Elegants
62	21	15	11	577	O ●	Stranger On The Shore [I]		2:52	Mr. Acker Bilk
58	18	15	11	578	O ●	Bird Dog		2:12	The Everly Brothers
76	28	22	10	579	O ●	A Fifth Of Beethoven [I]		3:02	Walter Murphy/ Big Apple Band
82	27	18	10	580	O ▲	Mickey		3:36	Toni Basil
93	23	18	10	581	O ●	A Whole New World (Aladdin's Theme)		3:58	Peabo Bryson & Regina Belle

YR	WEEKS			RANK	G O L D	PEAK POSITION	PEAK WEEKS	S Y M	TIME	ARTIST
	CH	40	10							
						Pos **1**^{1} Wks Cont'd				
81	26	17	10	582	O	● The Tide Is High................			3:50	Blondie
76	25	16	10	583	O	▲ Disco Duck (Part 1)............ [N]			3:15	Rick Dees & His Cast Of Idiots
78	22	16	10	584	O	● If I Can't Have You...............			2:57	Yvonne Elliman
76	20	16	10	585	O	● I Write The Songs................			3:39	Barry Manilow
57	23	15	10	586	O	● Party Doll......................			2:12	Buddy Knox
69	17	15	10	587	O	● Leaving On A Jet Plane...........			3:27	Peter, Paul & Mary
95	20	14	10	588	O	▲ You Are Not Alone...............			4:53	Michael Jackson
83	20	14	10	589	O	● Let's Dance.....................			4:08	David Bowie
75	17	14	10	590	O	One Of These Nights..............			3:28	Eagles
72	16	14	10	591	O	● Brandy (You're A Fine Girl)........			2:55	Looking Glass
76	16	14	10	592	O	● Love Rollercoaster...............			2:52	Ohio Players
70	17	13	10	593	O	● Make It With You................			3:14	Bread
81	20	20	9	594	O	▲ Keep On Loving You..............			3:22	REO Speedwagon
79	24	20	9	595	O	● Pop Muzik......................			3:20	M
79	27	19	9	596	O	● Sad Eyes.....................			3:30	Robert John
78	31	18	9	597	O	▲ Hot Child In The City............			3:06	Nick Gilder
90	25	18	9	598	O	● Hold On			3:32	Wilson Phillips
82	27	17	9	599	O	Who Can It Be Now?..............			3:20	Men At Work
83	26	17	9	600	O	● Sweet Dreams (Are Made of This)....			3:36	Eurythmics
91	24	17	9	601	O	● More Than Words.................			4:05	Extreme
91	23	17	9	602	O	● I Like The Way (The Kissing Game)...			3:42	Hi-Five
91	25	16	9	603	O	▲ One More Try			3:24	Timmy -T-
78	24	16	9	604	O	▲ You're The One That I Want			2:49	John Travolta & Olivia Newton-John
84	24	16	9	605	O	Missing You			3:58	John Waite
91	23	16	9	606	O	● Unbelievable			3:30	EMF
57	22	16	9	607	O	● That'll Be The Day..............			2:14	The Crickets
85	21	16	9	608	O	Separate Lives..................			4:06	Phil Collins & Marilyn Martin
91	20	16	9	609	O	When A Man Loves A Woman			3:40	Michael Bolton
78	20	16	9	610	O	● Miss You.....................			3:31	The Rolling Stones
70	19	16	9	611	O	I Want You Back.................			2:44	The Jackson 5
74	18	16	9	612	O	▲ Bennie And The Jets			5:20	Elton John
69	16	16	9	613	O	● Come Together.................			4:16	The Beatles
82	28	15	9	614	O	Chariots Of Fire - Titles........... [I]			3:15	Vangelis
71	22	15	9	615	O	▲ Indian Reservation (The Lament Of The Cherokee Reservation Indian)..			2:55	Raiders
77	18	15	9	616	O	Got To Give It Up (Pt. I)			3:58	Marvin Gaye
69	16	15	9	617	O	Someday We'll Be Together........			3:30	Diana Ross & The Supremes
72	16	15	9	618	O	● Let's Stay Together			3:15	Al Green
58	16	15	9	619	O	● Yakety Yak			1:50	The Coasters
77	23	14	9	620	O	▲ Car Wash			3:18	Rose Royce
85	21	14	9	621	O	● Crazy For You.................			4:08	Madonna
79	20	14	9	622	O	● What A Fool Believes.............			3:41	The Doobie Brothers
79	19	14	9	623	O	● Good Times...................			3:42	Chic
67	16	14	9	624	O	● Incense And Peppermints.........			2:37	Strawberry Alarm Clock
64	15	14	9	625	O	Mr. Lonely....................			2:37	Bobby Vinton
62	17	13	9	626	O	● The Stripper .... [I]			1:57	David Rose & His Orch.
79	15	13	9	627	O	● Heartache Tonight			4:26	Eagles
70	14	13	9	628	O	● Venus.......................			3:05	The Shocking Blue
59	16	12	9	629	O	Why			2:30	Frankie Avalon
66	15	12	9	630	O	● 96 Tears			2:38	? & The Mysterians

YR	WEEKS			RANK	G O L D	PEAK POSITION	PEAK WEEKS	S Y M	TIME	ARTIST
	CH	40	10							
						Pos **1** Wks ¹ Cont'd				
66	15	12	9	631	O ●	Last Train To Clarksville............			2:40	The Monkees
68	13	12	9	632	O ●	Harper Valley P.T.A................			3:12	Jeannie C. Riley
77	26	18	8	633	O ●	You Don't Have To Be A Star (To Be In My Show)..............			3:40	Marilyn McCoo & Billy Davis, Jr.
91	20	18	8	634	O ●	Set Adrift On Memory Bliss.........			3:53	PM Dawn
78	26	17	8	635	O ●	You Needed Me			3:38	Anne Murray
88	25	17	8	636	O	Need You Tonight			3:01	INXS
77	24	17	8	637	O	Don't Leave Me This Way...........			3:35	Thelma Houston
77	21	17	8	638	O ●	You Make Me Feel Like Dancing			2:48	Leo Sayer
87	22	16	8	639	O ▲	Shake You Down			4:04	Gregory Abbott
73	21	16	8	640	O	Touch Me In The Morning			3:51	Diana Ross
92	20	16	8	641	O ●	Don't Let The Sun Go Down On Me ..			5:44	George Michael/ Elton John
74	20	16	8	642	O ●	The Joker........................			3:36	Steve Miller Band
85	23	15	8	643	O ●	Everytime You Go Away...........			4:10	Paul Young
77	22	15	8	644	O ●	Dancing Queen			3:50	Abba
86	22	15	8	645	O	The Way It Is....................			4:57	Bruce Hornsby & The Range
88	22	15	8	646	O	Got My Mind Set On You			3:50	George Harrison
89	21	15	8	647	O ●	Cold Hearted			3:34	Paula Abdul
75	21	15	8	648	O ●	Before The Next Teardrop Falls			2:32	Freddy Fender
77	21	15	8	649	O ●	Southern Nights..................			2:58	Glen Campbell
77	20	15	8	650	O ●	Blinded By The Light..............			3:48	Manfred Mann's Earth Band
77	19	15	8	651	O ●	Hotel California			6:08	Eagles
74	19	15	8	652	O ●	Then Came You			3:53	Dionne Warwicke & The Spinners
77	17	15	8	653	O	I Wish			4:10	Stevie Wonder
75	23	14	8	654	O ●	My Eyes Adored You			3:25	Frankie Valli
85	22	14	8	655	O	Don't You (Forget About Me)........			4:20	Simple Minds
72	22	14	8	656	O ●	I Am Woman.....................			3:04	Helen Reddy
81	21	14	8	657	O ●	Medley			4:05	Stars on 45
85	21	14	8	658	O	Part-Time Lover			3:43	Stevie Wonder
90	21	14	8	659	O ▲	Blaze Of Glory			5:30	Jon Bon Jovi
92	20	14	8	660	O ●	This Used To Be My Playground			5:02	Madonna
73	20	14	8	661	O ●	Delta Dawn......................			3:08	Helen Reddy
90	19	14	8	662	O ●	I'm Your Baby Tonight			4:54	Whitney Houston
88	19	14	8	663	O ●	So Emotional			3:46	Whitney Houston
81	19	14	8	664	O ●	The One That You Love			4:07	Air Supply
72	15	14	8	665	O	I'll Take You There...............			3:19	The Staple Singers
77	20	13	8	666	O ●	Gonna Fly Now .... [I]			2:45	Bill Conti
89	18	13	8	667	O ●	Don't Wanna Lose You..............			4:10	Gloria Estefan
75	18	13	8	668	O ●	Lovin' You......................			3:20	Minnie Riperton
71	16	13	8	669	O ●	Want Ads			2:34	The Honey Cone
64	15	13	8	670	O ●	Everybody Loves Somebody........			2:40	Dean Martin
60	15	13	8	671	O ●	Itsy Bitsy Teenie Weenie Yellow Polkadot Bikini .... [N]			2:19	Brian Hyland
72	14	13	8	672	O ●	Heart Of Gold..................			2:59	Neil Young
60	15	12	8	673	O ●	Alley-Oop.................. [N]			2:36	Hollywood Argyles
61	14	12	8	674	O ●	Mother-In-Law			2:25	Ernie K-Doe
71	14	12	8	675	O ●	You've Got A Friend..............			4:26	James Taylor
78	18	11	8	676	O ●	Too Much, Too Little, Too Late			3:00	Johnny Mathis/ Deniece Williams
65	13	11	8	677	O	My Girl			2:55	The Temptations
64	12	11	8	678	O	A World Without Love			2:38	Peter & Gordon
91	20	19	7	679	O	Romantic			3:48	Karyn White

YR	WEEKS			RANK	G O L D	PEAK POSITION	PEAK WEEKS	S Y M	TIME	ARTIST
	CH	40	10							

Pos **1** ¹ Wks Cont'd

YR	CH	40	10	RANK	GOLD	PEAK POSITION		TIME	ARTIST
90	30	17	7	680	O ●	Close To You		3:55	Maxi Priest
77	25	17	7	681	O ●	Undercover Angel		3:24	Alan O'Day
88	27	16	7	682	O ●	Wild, Wild West		3:59	The Escape Club
74	22	16	7	683	O ●	Love's Theme	[I]	3:30	Love Unlimited Orchestra
74	22	16	7	684	O ●	Show And Tell		3:28	Al Wilson
89	29	15	7	685	O ▲	Wind Beneath My Wings		4:54	Bette Midler
85	27	15	7	686	O ●	Take On Me		3:46	a-ha
90	26	15	7	687	O	I Don't Have The Heart		3:52	James Ingram
89	24	15	7	688	O ●	My Prerogative		4:25	Bobby Brown
61	23	15	7	689	O ●	Please Mr. Postman		2:20	The Marvelettes
91	22	15	7	690	O ●	Love Will Never Do (Without You)		4:26	Janet Jackson
85	22	15	7	691	O ●	Saving All My Love For You		3:48	Whitney Houston
90	21	15	7	692	O ▲	Ice Ice Baby		4:53	Vanilla Ice
76	21	15	7	693	O ●	Boogie Fever		3:25	Sylvers
91	20	15	7	694	O ●	Good Vibrations		4:26	Marky Mark & Funky Bunch
86	20	15	7	695	O	Human		3:46	Human League
75	20	15	7	696	O	Laughter In The Rain		2:50	Neil Sedaka
83	18	15	7	697	O	Tell Her About It		3:35	Billy Joel
87	28	14	7	698	O	Here I Go Again		3:52	Whitesnake
90	26	14	7	699	O ●	(Can't Live Without Your) Love And Affection		3:47	Nelson
89	23	14	7	700	O ●	She Drives Me Crazy		3:35	Fine Young Cannibals
86	22	14	7	701	O ●	Addicted To Love		3:59	Robert Palmer
87	22	14	7	702	O	Always		3:59	Atlantic Starr
79	21	14	7	703	O ●	Heart Of Glass		3:22	Blondie
86	21	14	7	704	O	There'll Be Sad Songs (To Make You Cry)		4:02	Billy Ocean
86	21	14	7	705	O	Sledgehammer		4:58	Peter Gabriel
86	20	14	7	706	O	West End Girls		3:55	Pet Shop Boys
77	20	14	7	707	O ●	When I Need You		4:11	Leo Sayer
87	20	14	7	708	O ●	Head To Toe		3:58	Lisa Lisa & Cult Jam
73	20	14	7	709	O ●	Frankenstein	[I]	3:28	The Edgar Winter Group
74	19	14	7	710	O	You Haven't Done Nothin		3:20	Stevie Wonder
91	19	14	7	711	O	You're In Love		3:58	Wilson Phillips
87	18	14	7	712	O	Shakedown		3:59	Bob Seger
74	18	14	7	713	O ●	Nothing From Nothing		2:40	Billy Preston
75	18	14	7	714	O ●	(Hey Won't You Play) Another Somebody Done Somebody Wrong Song		3:23	B.J. Thomas
59	17	14	7	715	O	The Happy Organ	[I]	2:01	Dave 'Baby' Cortez
74	17	14	7	716	O ●	Hooked On A Feeling		2:54	Blue Swede
70	15	14	7	717	O ▲	Cracklin' Rosie		2:47	Neil Diamond
72	15	14	7	718	O	Oh Girl		3:16	Chi-Lites
85	22	13	7	719	O	Miami Vice Theme	[I]	2:26	Jan Hammer
86	21	13	7	720	O ●	Take My Breath Away		4:13	Berlin
80	21	13	7	721	O	Sailing		4:15	Christopher Cross
90	20	13	7	722	O	If Wishes Came True		5:09	Sweet Sensation
86	20	13	7	723	O	Sara		4:18	Starship
77	19	13	7	724	O ●	Don't Give Up On Us		3:30	David Soul
89	19	13	7	725	O ●	The Look		3:56	Roxette
77	19	13	7	726	O ●	Dreams		4:14	Fleetwood Mac
74	18	13	7	727	O ●	Sunshine On My Shoulders		3:18	John Denver
74	18	13	7	728	O ●	Band On The Run		5:09	Paul McCartney & Wings
75	18	13	7	729	O ●	Lady Marmalade		3:14	LaBelle
73	17	13	7	730	O	You Are The Sunshine Of My Life		3:00	Stevie Wonder

YR	WEEKS			RANK	G O L D	PEAK POSITION	PEAK WEEKS	S Y M	TIME	ARTIST
	CH	40	10							

Pos **1** ^{1} Wks Cont'd

YR	CH	40	10	RANK	GOLD	PEAK POSITION	PEAK WEEKS	TIME	ARTIST
75	17	13	7	731	O ●	Pick Up The Pieces . . . . [I]		3:00	AWB
76	17	13	7	732	O	Theme From Mahogany (Do You Know Where You're Going To)		3:19	Diana Ross
73	16	13	7	733	O ●	Angie		4:30	The Rolling Stones
77	15	13	7	734	O ●	New Kid In Town.		4:49	Eagles
77	22	12	7	735	O ●	Da Doo Ron Ron		2:46	Shaun Cassidy
76	20	12	7	736	O ●	You Should Be Dancing.		4:15	Bee Gees
86	19	12	7	737	O	Venus.		3:49	Bananarama
76	19	12	7	738	O	Let Your Love Flow		3:16	Bellamy Brothers
75	19	12	7	739	O ●	The Hustle. . . . . [I]		3:27	Van McCoy
75	17	12	7	740	O ●	Black Water		4:17	The Doobie Brothers
62	16	12	7	741	O ●	The Loco-Motion		2:12	Little Eva
61	16	12	7	742	O ●	Wooden Heart		2:00	Joe Dowell
74	15	12	7	743	O ●	You're Sixteen		2:50	Ringo Starr
75	15	12	7	744	O ●	Let's Do It Again		3:28	The Staple Singers
66	15	12	7	745	O	Poor Side Of Town		3:03	Johnny Rivers
63	15	12	7	746	O	So Much In Love		2:08	The Tymes
63	15	12	7	747	O	Deep Purple		2:41	Nino Tempo & April Stevens
66	14	12	7	748	O ●	These Boots Are Made For Walkin' . . .		2:40	Nancy Sinatra
66	14	12	7	749	O ●	Good Vibrations.		3:35	The Beach Boys
66	14	12	7	750	O	Good Lovin'		2:28	The Young Rascals
71	13	12	7	751	O ●	Uncle Albert/Admiral Halsey		4:47	Paul & Linda McCartney
68	13	12	7	752	O ●	Green Tambourine		2:22	The Lemon Pipers
74	18	11	7	753	O ●	Sundown		3:37	Gordon Lightfoot
72	16	11	7	754	O	Ben.		2:42	Michael Jackson
75	16	11	7	755	O ●	Have You Never Been Mellow		3:28	Olivia Newton-John
76	16	11	7	756	O	Convoy. . . . . [N]		3:48	C.W. McCall
66	15	11	7	757	O ●	Strangers In The Night.		2:35	Frank Sinatra
75	14	11	7	758	O ●	Listen To What The Man Said.		3:53	Wings
76	14	11	7	759	O ●	Welcome Back		2:48	John Sebastian
73	14	11	7	760	O	Give Me Love - (Give Me Peace On Earth).		3:32	George Harrison
65	14	11	7	761	O	Hang On Sloopy.		2:57	The McCoys
60	13	10	7	762	O	Mr. Custer . . . . [N]		2:59	Larry Verne
66	13	10	7	763	O	Sunshine Superman		3:11	Donovan
65	13	10	7	764	O	Mr. Tambourine Man.		2:18	The Byrds
64	12	10	7	765	O	Ringo . . . . [S]		3:00	Lorne Greene
67	11	10	7	766	O	Love Is Here And Now You're Gone . .		2:35	The Supremes
65	11	10	7	767	O	Eve Of Destruction		3:28	Barry McGuire
67	12	9	7	768	O ●	Ruby Tuesday.		3:12	The Rolling Stones
67	11	9	7	769	O ●	All You Need Is Love		3:57	The Beatles
76	28	19	6	770	O	Love Machine (Part 1)		2:55	The Miracles
88	40	16	6	771	O ●	Red Red Wine.		5:21	UB40
77	23	16	6	772	O	I'm Your Boogie Man		3:58	KC & The Sunshine Band
83	21	16	6	773	O ●	Africa		4:23	Toto
88	20	16	6	774	O	Seasons Change		3:58	Exposé
88	25	15	6	775	O ●	Wishing Well		3:33	Terence Trent D'Arby
88	24	15	6	776	O ●	Baby, I Love Your Way/Freebird Medley (Free Baby)		4:07	Will To Power
89	22	15	6	777	O ●	If You Don't Know Me By Now		3:24	Simply Red
87	21	15	6	778	O	Heaven Is A Place On Earth		3:49	Belinda Carlisle
87	21	15	6	779	O ●	(I've Had) The Time Of My Life		4:47	Bill Medley & Jennifer Warnes
86	21	15	6	780	O	The Next Time I Fall		3:43	Peter Cetera w/Amy Grant

TEQUILA

By CHUCK RIO

Recorded by THE CHAMPS — Challenge Record No. 1016
Also recorded by STAN KENTON — Capitol Record No. 3928

60 cents

JAT MUSIC COMPANY
Selling Agent

KEYS-HANSEN, INC.
119 W. 57th Street
New York 19, N. Y.

YR	CH	40	10	RANK	GOLD	PEAK POSITION	PEAK WEEKS	SYM	TIME	ARTIST

Pos 1 ¹ Wks Cont'd

YR	CH	40	10	RANK	GOLD		SYM	TITLE	TIME	ARTIST
90	20	15	6	781	O	●		Love Will Lead You Back	4:18	Taylor Dayne
86	24	14	6	782	O			You Give Love A Bad Name	3:53	Bon Jovi
83	23	14	6	783	O			Come On Eileen	4:12	Dexys Midnight Runners
86	23	14	6	784	O			Holding Back The Years	4:04	Simply Red
86	22	14	6	785	O			Higher Love	4:08	Steve Winwood
89	22	14	6	786	O			Listen To Your Heart	5:26	Roxette
89	21	14	6	787	O	●		I'll Be Loving You (Forever)	3:54	New Kids On The Block
88	21	14	6	788	O			Hold On To The Nights	4:34	Richard Marx
89	21	14	6	789	O	●		Baby Don't Forget My Number	4:01	Milli Vanilli
79	20	14	6	790	O	▲		Knock On Wood	3:40	Amii Stewart
89	20	14	6	791	O			The Living Years	5:30	Mike & The Mechanics
88	20	14	6	792	O			Foolish Beat	4:20	Debbie Gibson
91	19	14	6	793	O			Joyride	3:53	Roxette
91	19	14	6	794	O	●		I've Been Thinking About You	3:40	Londonbeat
75	19	14	6	795	O			Best Of My Love	3:25	The Eagles
89	19	14	6	796	O	●		Eternal Flame	3:56	Bangles
87	18	14	6	797	O			Open Your Heart	4:12	Madonna
85	17	14	6	798	O	●		Sussudio	4:23	Phil Collins
88	23	13	6	799	O			Love Bites	5:46	Def Leppard
89	22	13	6	800	O			I'll Be There For You	5:43	Bon Jovi
85	21	13	6	801	O			Oh Sheila	3:36	Ready For The World
87	21	13	6	802	O			You Keep Me Hangin' On	4:13	Kim Wilde
86	20	13	6	803	O			These Dreams	3:46	Heart
87	20	13	6	804	O	●		Lost In Emotion	3:59	Lisa Lisa & Cult Jam
74	18	13	6	805	O	●		Rock Me Gently	3:28	Andy Kim
86	18	13	6	806	O			Live To Tell	4:37	Madonna
88	18	13	6	807	O			The Way You Make Me Feel	4:26	Michael Jackson
74	17	13	6	808	O	●		Angie Baby	3:29	Helen Reddy
73	17	13	6	809	O	●		We're An American Band	3:25	Grand Funk
89	17	13	6	810	O			Good Thing	3:22	Fine Young Cannibals
73	16	13	6	811	O			Superstition	3:59	Stevie Wonder
74	16	13	6	812	O	●		Feel Like Makin' Love	2:55	Roberta Flack
60	15	13	6	813	O			I Want To Be Wanted	3:00	Brenda Lee
69	15	13	6	814	O	▲		Suspicious Minds	4:22	Elvis Presley
73	14	13	6	815	O	●		Love Train	2:59	O'Jays
76	24	12	6	816	O	●		Theme From S.W.A.T. [I]	2:47	Rhythm Heritage
87	22	12	6	817	O			Mony Mony "Live"	4:00	Billy Idol
79	21	12	6	818	O	▲		Don't Stop 'Til You Get Enough	5:56	Michael Jackson
74	19	12	6	819	O	●		Cat's In The Cradle	3:29	Harry Chapin
88	18	12	6	820	O			Together Forever	3:20	Rick Astley
76	17	12	6	821	O	●		Saturday Night	2:56	Bay City Rollers
86	17	12	6	822	O			Invisible Touch	3:26	Genesis
75	17	12	6	823	O	●		Fallin' In Love	3:13	Hamilton, Joe Frank & Reynolds
89	17	12	6	824	O	▲		Hangin' Tough	3:51	New Kids On The Block
73	16	12	6	825	O	●		Photograph	3:59	Ringo Starr
74	16	12	6	826	O	●		Dark Lady	3:26	Cher
72	16	12	6	827	O			Papa Was A Rollin' Stone	6:58	The Temptations
61	15	12	6	828	O			Moody River	2:38	Pat Boone
87	15	12	6	829	O			Jacob's Ladder	3:28	Huey Lewis & the News
72	13	12	6	830	O	●		Song Sung Blue	3:15	Neil Diamond
89	18	11	6	831	O	▲		Batdance	4:06	Prince
74	17	11	6	832	O	●		The Night Chicago Died	3:30	Paper Lace
87	16	11	6	833	O			Who's That Girl	3:58	Madonna

YR	WEEKS			RANK	G O L D	PEAK POSITION	PEAK WEEKS	S Y M	TIME	ARTIST
	CH	40	10							

Pos 1 — 1 Wks — Cont'd

YR	CH	40	10	RANK	GOLD	SONG		SYM	TIME	ARTIST
64	14	11	6	834	O	Love Me Do			2:18	The Beatles
87	14	11	6	835	O ●	I Just Can't Stop Loving You			4:17	Michael Jackson
65	12	11	6	836	O	Over And Over			2:00	The Dave Clark Five
66	15	10	6	837	O ●	Lightnin' Strikes			2:44	Lou Christie
90	14	10	6	838	O	Praying For Time			4:30	George Michael
63	13	10	6	839	O	Our Day Will Come			2:31	Ruby & The Romantics
62	13	10	6	840	O	Don't Break The Heart That Loves You			2:58	Connie Francis
67	11	10	6	841	O	The Happening			2:50	The Supremes
65	11	9	6	842	O	Ticket To Ride			3:02	The Beatles
65	10	8	6	843	O ●	I'm Henry VIII, I Am			1:49	Herman's Hermits
88	28	15	5	844	O ▲	Kokomo			3:34	The Beach Boys
75	19	15	5	845	O ●	Thank God I'm A Country Boy			2:47	John Denver
75	20	14	5	846	O ●	Shining Star			2:50	Earth, Wind & Fire
76	18	14	5	847	O	Rock'n Me			3:05	Steve Miller
60	18	14	5	848	O	Stay			1:50	Maurice Williams & Zodiacs
89	28	13	5	849	O ●	When I'm With You			3:54	Sheriff
89	21	13	5	850	O ●	Rock On			3:21	Michael Damian
77	19	13	5	851	O ●	Looks Like We Made It			3:29	Barry Manilow
79	19	13	5	852	O ●	Love You Inside Out			3:48	Bee Gees
90	18	13	5	853	O ●	I'll Be Your Everything			3:58	Tommy Page
91	16	13	5	854	O	The Promise Of A New Day			4:09	Paula Abdul
89	15	13	5	855	O	Satisfied			3:58	Richard Marx
74	17	12	5	856	O ●	You Ain't Seen Nothing Yet			3:29	Bachman-Turner Overdrive
75	17	12	5	857	O ●	Please Mr. Postman			2:48	Carpenters
75	16	12	5	858	O ●	Mandy			3:15	Barry Manilow
90	16	12	5	859	O ●	Black Cat			4:25	Janet Jackson
88	14	11	5	860	O	Dirty Diana			4:37	Michael Jackson
74	18	10	5	861	O ●	Rock The Boat			3:03	The Hues Corporation
75	16	10	5	862	O	You're No Good			3:40	Linda Ronstadt
74	14	10	5	863	O ●	I Shot The Sheriff			3:30	Eric Clapton
60	13	10	5	864	O	Georgia On My Mind			3:37	Ray Charles
64	12	10	5	865	O	Leader Of The Pack			2:48	The Shangri-Las
65	11	10	5	866	O	Game Of Love			2:04	Wayne Fontana/ Mindbenders
65	11	10	5	867	O	Back In My Arms Again			2:50	The Supremes
72	11	9	5	868	O ●	Black & White			3:24	Three Dog Night
67	10	9	5	869	O ●	Penny Lane			3:00	The Beatles
61	17	15	4	870	O	Running Scared			2:10	Roy Orbison
75	18	13	4	871	O ●	I'm Sorry			3:29	John Denver
75	17	12	4	872	O ●	Fire			3:12	Ohio Players
75	16	12	4	873	O	Sister Golden Hair			3:16	America
75	15	9	4	874	O	Get Down Tonight			3:21	K.C. & The Sunshine Band
74	12	9	4	875	O ●	Can't Get Enough Of Your Love, Babe			3:15	Barry White
74	15	11	3	876	O	Whatever Gets You Thru The Night			3:20	John Lennon/ Plastic Ono Band

Pos 2 — 10 Wks

YR	CH	40	10	RANK	GOLD	SONG	SYM	TIME	ARTIST
81	23	19	15	877	O ●	Waiting For A Girl Like You		4:35	Foreigner

Pos 2 — 9 Wks

YR	CH	40	10	RANK	GOLD	SONG	SYM	TIME	ARTIST
96	41	35	16	878	O ●	I Love You Always Forever		3:56	Donna Lewis

YR	WEEKS			RANK	G O L D	PEAK POSITION	PEAK WEEKS	S Y M	TIME	ARTIST
	CH	40	10							

Pos 2 — 8 Wks

YR	CH	40	10	RANK	GOLD			TIME	ARTIST
92	27	24	15	879 O	▲	If I Ever Fall In Love		3:05	Shai
57	26	21	14	880 O	●	Little Darlin'		2:05	The Diamonds

Pos 2 — 7 Wks

93	45	41	24	881 O	▲⁴	Whoomp! (There It Is)		4:27	Tag Team
55	20	20	16	882 O	●	The Crazy Otto . . . . [I]		2:58	Johnny Maddox

Pos 2 — 6 Wks

55	25	25	19	883 O	●	Moments To Remember		3:14	The Four Lads
94	33	27	14	884 O	●	All I Wanna Do		4:06	Sheryl Crow
92	33	24	14	885 O	▲	Baby-Baby-Baby		4:05	TLC
92	24	20	11	886 O	●	Sometimes Love Just Ain't Enough . .		4:26	Patty Smyth with Don Henley
82	18	14	10	887 O		Open Arms		3:21	Journey
78	20	15	9	888 O	●	Baker Street		4:08	Gerry Rafferty
63	18	13	9	889 O		Louie Louie		2:24	The Kingsmen

Pos 2 — 5 Wks

82	23	18	11	890 O	●	Rosanna		3:59	Toto
62	16	14	10	891 O	▲	Return To Sender		2:05	Elvis Presley
80	23	15	9	892 O	●	More Than I Can Say		3:40	Leo Sayer
83	22	15	8	893 O	▲	Electric Avenue		3:47	Eddy Grant

Pos 2 — 4 Wks

57	38	26	18	894 O	●	So Rare		2:30	Jimmy Dorsey
82	28	22	16	895 O	●	Hurts So Good		3:35	John Cougar
57	27	22	15	896 O	●	Bye Bye Love		2:17	The Everly Brothers
56	24	19	14	897 O	●	No, Not Much!		3:12	The Four Lads
92	26	23	12	898 O	▲	Tears In Heaven		4:29	Eric Clapton
95	25	21	12	899 O	●	Candy Rain		4:28	Soul For Real
91	22	19	11	900 O	●	It's So Hard To Say Goodbye To Yesterday		2:45	Boyz II Men

56	21	17	11	901 O		Blue Suede Shoes		2:14	Carl Perkins
82	21	16	11	902 O		Don't Talk To Strangers		3:00	Rick Springfield
94	26	24	10	903 O	●	I'll Remember		4:13	Madonna
80	27	17	10	904 O	●	All Out Of Love		3:51	Air Supply
91	23	16	10	905 O	▲²	I Wanna Sex You Up		4:09	Color Me Badd
60	20	15	10	906 O	●	Last Date . . . . [I]		2:20	Floyd Cramer
83	18	15	10	907 O		Say It Isn't So		3:56	Daryl Hall & John Oates
80	21	17	9	908 O		Ride Like The Wind		3:54	Christopher Cross
84	21	15	9	909 O	▲	Dancing In The Dark		3:59	Bruce Springsteen
60	20	15	9	910 O		Greenfields		3:00	The Brothers Four
70	17	14	9	911 O	●	We've Only Just Begun		3:09	Carpenters
58	21	13	9	912 O	●	Great Balls Of Fire		1:50	Jerry Lee Lewis
83	21	19	8	913 O		Shame On The Moon		4:55	Bob Seger & Silver Bullet Band
84	18	14	8	914 O	●	The Wild Boys		4:14	Duran Duran
66	12	11	8	915 O	●	Snoopy Vs. The Red Baron . . . . [N]		2:43	The Royal Guardsmen
64	26	16	7	916 O		Twist And Shout		2:33	The Beatles
63	15	12	7	917 O		Can't Get Used To Losing You		2:19	Andy Williams
68	13	11	7	918 O		(Theme From) Valley Of The Dolls		3:35	Dionne Warwick
87	19	14	6	919 O		Looking For A New Love		3:58	Jody Watley
73	14	11	6	920 O	●	Dueling Banjos . . . . [I]		3:17	Eric Weissberg & Steve Mandell

YR	WEEKS			RANK	G O L D	PEAK POSITION	PEAK WEEKS	S Y M	TIME	ARTIST
	CH	40	10							
						Pos **2** **3** Wks				
75	10	7	5	921	O	Calypso			3:32	John Denver
93	36	30	18	922	O	▲ All That She Wants			3:27	Ace Of Base
56	39	22	16	923	O	● Honky Tonk (Parts 1 & 2)	[I]		5:35	Bill Doggett
57	27	21	16	924	O	● Blueberry Hill			2:14	Fats Domino
92	28	23	15	925	O	▲² Rump Shaker			3:51	Wreckx-N-Effect
56	27	22	15	926	O	● Whatever Will Be, Will Be (Que Sera, Sera)			2:01	Doris Day
95	29	27	14	927	O	▲ Don't Take It Personal (just one of dem days)			4:12	Monica
55	18	17	14	928	O	● I Hear You Knocking			2:20	Gale Storm
92	30	22	13	929	O	● My Lovin' (You're Never Gonna Get It)			4:32	En Vogue
79	26	20	12	930	O	▲ Y.M.C.A.			3:42	Village People
60	23	20	12	931	O	● He'll Have To Go			2:16	Jim Reeves
95	22	19	12	932	O	● Red Light Special			4:53	TLC
81	20	17	12	933	O	● Woman			3:30	John Lennon
92	26	21	11	934	O	I Love Your Smile			4:19	Shanice
81	24	19	11	935	O	Start Me Up			3:32	The Rolling Stones
94	20	18	11	936	O	▲ Regulate			4:05	Warren G. & Nate Dogg
81	24	16	11	937	O	● Slow Hand			3:57	Pointer Sisters
81	24	16	11	938	O	Just The Two Of Us			3:56	Grover Washington, Jr. (with Bill Withers)
59	18	14	11	939	O	Put Your Head On My Shoulder			2:39	Paul Anka
82	36	22	10	940	O	▲ Gloria			4:50	Laura Branigan
77	26	18	10	941	O	● Don't It Make My Brown Eyes Blue			2:37	Crystal Gayle
95	20	17	10	942	O	▲ One More Chance/Stay With Me			4:14	The Notorious B.I.G.
81	20	17	10	943	O	Love On The Rocks			3:41	Neil Diamond
81	25	16	10	944	O	● Being With You			3:58	Smokey Robinson
59	19	14	10	945	O	● Personality			2:35	Lloyd Price
83	18	14	10	946	O	● The Girl Is Mine			3:41	Michael Jackson/ Paul McCartney
93	22	19	9	947	O	● Right Here/Human Nature			3:44	SWV-Sisters With Voices
83	25	18	9	948	O	Do You Really Want To Hurt Me			4:23	Culture Club
83	25	17	9	949	O	● Making Love Out Of Nothing At All			4:29	Air Supply
76	21	17	9	950	O	● The Rubberband Man			3:30	Spinners
76	21	15	9	951	O	● Get Up And Boogie (That's Right)			4:05	Silver Convention
82	19	15	9	952	O	● We Got The Beat			2:30	Go-Go's
85	22	14	9	953	O	▲ Party All The Time			3:58	Eddie Murphy
67	17	14	9	954	O	I Heard It Through The Grapevine			2:52	Gladys Knight & The Pips
55	14	14	9	955	O	Ko Ko Mo (I Love You So)			2:37	Perry Como
69	15	12	9	956	O	Crystal Blue Persuasion			3:45	Tommy James & The Shondells
77	25	15	8	957	O	● Nobody Does It Better			3:30	Carly Simon
76	20	14	8	958	O	● Dream Weaver			3:15	Gary Wright
58	20	14	8	959	O	● 26 Miles (Santa Catalina)			2:31	The Four Preps
84	19	14	8	960	O	● Somebody's Watching Me			3:57	Rockwell
58	18	14	8	961	O	● Stood Up			1:57	Ricky Nelson
68	15	13	8	962	O	● Young Girl			3:12	Union Gap feat. Gary Puckett
71	15	13	8	963	O	What's Going On			3:40	Marvin Gaye
61	16	12	8	964	O	The Boll Weevil Song	[N]		2:35	Brook Benton
59	15	12	8	965	O	● Charlie Brown	[N]		2:12	The Coasters
67	15	11	8	966	O	● Soul Man			2:36	Sam & Dave
85	25	15	7	967	O	● Cherish			3:58	Kool & The Gang
77	20	14	7	968	O	Keep It Comin' Love			3:48	KC & The Sunshine Band
73	17	14	7	969	O	▲ Goodbye Yellow Brick Road			3:13	Elton John
68	14	12	7	970	O	● Those Were The Days			5:05	Mary Hopkin

YR	WEEKS			RANK	G O L D		PEAK POSITION	PEAK WEEKS		S Y M	TIME	ARTIST
	CH	40	10									

Pos **2**³ _{Wks} Cont'd

YR	CH	40	10	RANK	GOLD		PEAK POSITION			SYM	TIME	ARTIST
69	14	12	7	971	O	▲	Proud Mary......................				3:07	Creedence Clearwater Revival
73	14	12	7	972	O	●	Live And Let Die				3:10	Wings
69	13	12	7	973	O	●	Spinning Wheel				2:39	Blood, Sweat & Tears
58	16	11	7	974	O		Sweet Little Sixteen..............				2:35	Chuck Berry
69	12	11	7	975	O	●	A Boy Named Sue			[N]	3:40	Johnny Cash
71	12	11	7	976	O		Never Can Say Goodbye				2:56	The Jackson 5
61	17	10	7	977	O		I Like It Like That, Part 1				1:55	Chris Kenner
66	12	10	7	978	O	●	Mellow Yellow....................				3:40	Donovan
90	21	14	6	979	O	●	Don't Wanna Fall In Love..........				4:04	Jane Child
76	19	14	6	980	O	●	All By Myself				4:22	Eric Carmen
89	20	13	6	981	O	▲	On Our Own.....................				4:30	Bobby Brown
77	20	13	6	982	O		I'm In You				4:08	Peter Frampton
88	19	13	6	983	O		Shattered Dreams				3:30	Johnny Hates Jazz
86	16	12	6	984	O		Typical Male....................				4:14	Tina Turner
68	14	12	6	985	O	●	The Horse			[I]	2:25	Cliff Nobles & Co.
68	13	12	6	986	O	●	Born To Be Wild				2:55	Steppenwolf
81	16	11	6	987	O		All Those Years Ago.............				3:42	George Harrison
65	15	11	6	988	O	●	A Lover's Concerto				2:36	The Toys
63	13	11	6	989	O		Ruby Baby				2:31	Dion
69	13	11	6	990	O	●	You've Made Me So Very Happy				3:26	Blood, Sweat & Tears
63	13	10	6	991	O		Be My Baby				2:20	The Ronettes
66	10	9	6	992	O		19th Nervous Breakdown				3:50	The Rolling Stones
67	10	9	6	993	O		Dedicated To The One I Love.......				2:56	The Mamas & The Papa
63	10	8	6	994	O		Hello Mudduh, Hello Fadduh! (A Letter From Camp)..........			[C]	2:47	Allan Sherman
78	20	13	5	995	O	●	Short People			[N]	2:54	Randy Newman
87	18	11	5	996	O		Causing A Commotion				4:00	Madonna
75	17	11	5	997	O		I'm Not In Love..................				3:40	10cc
64	13	10	5	998	O		You Don't Own Me				2:26	Lesley Gore

Pos **2**² _{Wks}

YR	CH	40	10	RANK	GOLD		PEAK POSITION			SYM	TIME	ARTIST
96	47	38	23	999	O	▲	Nobody Knows..................				4:22	The Tony Rich Project
56	31	23	14	1000	O	●	Canadian Sunset...............			[I]	2:50	Hugo Winterhalter & His Orch. w/ Eddie Heywoo

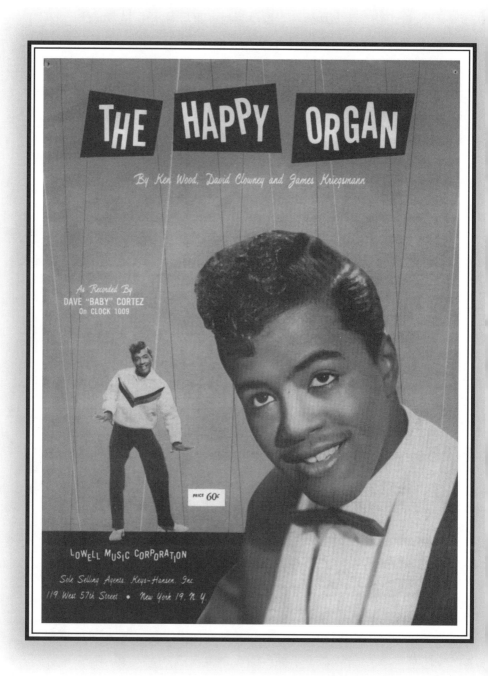

THE YEARS

his section lists each year's Top 40 hits. These rankings are based on the Top
000 ranking system.

ou will find hundreds of additional hits in these yearly Top 40 rankings that do not
ppear in the Top 1000 ranking. A break separates the Top 1000-ranked titles from
ose that do not rank within the Top 1000.

Columnar headings show the following data:

RANK:	Top 1000 ranking
PK DATE:	Date title reached its peak position
PK WKS:	Total weeks title held its peak position
PK POS:	Highest charted position title attained

TOP 40 HITS
1955

RANK	PK DATE	PK WKS	PK POS	TITLE	ARTIST
9	4/30	10	1	1. Cherry Pink And Apple Blossom White	Perez Prado & His Orch.
10	2/12	10	1	2. Sincerely	The McGuire Sisters
20	7/09	8	1	3. (We're Gonna) Rock Around The Clock	Bill Haley & His Comets
23	11/26	8	1	4. Sixteen Tons	"Tennessee" Ernie Ford
54	10/08	6	1	5. Love Is A Many-Splendored Thing	Four Aces
57	9/03	6	1	6. The Yellow Rose Of Texas	Mitch Miller Chorus
81	3/26	5	1	7. The Ballad Of Davy Crockett	Bill Hayes
120	10/29	4	1	8. Autumn Leaves	Roger Williams
140	1/01	4	1	9. Let Me Go Lover	Joan Weber
202	5/14	3	1	10. Dance With Me Henry (Wallflower)	Georgia Gibbs
206	2/05	3	1	11. Hearts Of Stone	The Fontane Sisters
326	5/14	2	1	12. Unchained Melody	Les Baxter Chorus
327	7/09	2	1	13. Learnin' The Blues	Frank Sinatra
333	9/17	2	1	14. Ain't That A Shame	Pat Boone
882	3/12	7	2	15. The Crazy Otto	Johnny Maddox
883	10/29	6	2	16. Moments To Remember	The Four Lads
928	12/10	3	2	17. I Hear You Knocking	Gale Storm
955	3/05	3	2	18. Ko Ko Mo (I Love You So)	Perry Como
	1/01	1	2	19. Teach Me Tonight	The DeCastro Sisters
	3/05	1	2	20. Melody Of Love	Billy Vaughn Orch.
	7/09	1	2	21. A Blossom Fell	Nat "King" Cole
	4/02	1	2	22. Tweedle Dee	Georgia Gibbs
	4/09	1	2	23. How Important Can It Be?	Joni James
	11/26	2	3	24. The Shifting, Whispering Sands	Rusty Draper
	6/04	1	3	25. Unchained Melody	Al Hibbler
	3/12	1	3	26. Melody Of Love	Four Aces Featuring Al Albe...
	9/17	1	3	27. The Yellow Rose Of Texas	Johnny Desmond
	10/08	1	3	28. Seventeen	The Fontane Sisters
	2/26	1	3	29. That's All I Want From You	Jaye P. Morgan
	3/12	1	3	30. Earth Angel	The Crew-Cuts
	8/13	1	4	31. Hard To Get	Gisele MacKenzie
	12/31	1	4	32. He	Al Hibbler
	5/14	4	5	33. Ballad Of Davy Crockett	"Tennessee" Ernie Ford
	10/22	4	5	34. The Shifting Whispering Sands (Parts 1 & 2)	Billy Vaughn Orch.
	11/05	3	5	35. Only You (And You Alone)	The Platters
	11/26	3	5	36. Love And Marriage	Frank Sinatra
	1/01	3	5	37. Mister Sandman	Four Aces Feat. Al Alberts
	5/21	1	5	38. Ballad Of Davy Crockett	Fess Parker
	10/15	1	5	39. Tina Marie	Perry Como
	7/23	1	5	40. Something's Gotta Give	The McGuire Sisters

TOP 40 HITS
1956

ANK	PK DATE	PK WKS	PK POS	TITLE	ARTIST
6	8/18	11	1	1. Don't Be Cruel /	Elvis Presley
7	8/18	11	1	2. Hound Dog	Elvis Presley
11	12/08	10	1	3. Singing The Blues	Guy Mitchell
22	6/16	8	1	4. The Wayward Wind	Gogi Grant
24	4/21	8	1	5. Heartbreak Hotel	Elvis Presley
55	2/18	6	1	6. Rock And Roll Waltz	Kay Starr
56	3/17	6	1	7. The Poor People Of Paris	Les Baxter & His Orch.
59	1/07	6	1	8. Memories Are Made Of This	Dean Martin
83	11/03	5	1	9. Love Me Tender	Elvis Presley
84	8/04	5	1	10. My Prayer	The Platters
121	2/25	4	1	11. Lisbon Antigua	Nelson Riddle & His Orch.
125	7/28	4	1	12. I Almost Lost My Mind	Pat Boone
199	11/03	3	1	13. The Green Door	Jim Lowe
203	6/02	3	1	14. Moonglow and Theme From "Picnic"	Morris Stoloff & His Orch.
336	2/18	2	1	15. The Great Pretender	The Platters
561	5/05	1	1	16. Hot Diggity (Dog Ziggity Boom)	Perry Como
563	7/28	1	1	17. I Want You, I Need You, I Love You	Elvis Presley
897	3/17	4	2	18. No, Not Much!	The Four Lads
901	5/19	4	2	19. Blue Suede Shoes	Carl Perkins
923	10/06	3	2	20. Honky Tonk (Parts 1 & 2)	Bill Doggett
926	8/18	3	2	21. Whatever Will Be, Will Be (Que Sera, Sera)	Doris Day
000	10/13	2	2	22. Canadian Sunset	Hugo Winterhalter/ Eddie Heywood
	8/18	2	2	23. Allegheny Moon	Patti Page
	10/27	1	2	24. Just Walking In The Rain	Johnnie Ray
	6/16	1	2	25. Ivory Tower	Cathy Carr
	6/16	3	3	26. Standing On The Corner	The Four Lads
	7/14	2	3	27. I'm In Love Again	Fats Domino
	11/10	1	3	28. True Love	Bing Crosby/Grace Kelly
	8/25	1	3	29. The Flying Saucer (Parts 1 & 2)	Buchanan & Goodman
	7/07	4	4	30. On The Street Where You Live	Vic Damone
	5/19	3	4	31. (You've Got) The Magic Touch	The Platters
	1/07	1	4	32. Band Of Gold	Don Cherry
	4/07	1	4	33. I'll Be Home	Pat Boone
	10/06	1	4	34. Tonight You Belong To Me	Patience & Prudence
	6/02	1	4	35. Moonglow And Theme From "Picnic"	George Cates
	7/21	1	4	36. More	Perry Como
	5/12	2	5	37. A Tear Fell	Teresa Brewer
	7/14	2	5	38. Born To Be With You	The Chordettes
	10/20	1	5	39. Friendly Persuasion (Thee I Love)	Pat Boone
	1/14	1	5	40. Memories Are Made Of This	Gale Storm

TOP 40 HITS
1957

RANK	PK DATE	PK WKS	PK POS	TITLE	ARTIST
15	4/13	9	1	1. All Shook Up	Elvis Presley
33	6/03	7	1	2. Love Letters In The Sand	Pat Boone
36	10/21	7	1	3. Jailhouse Rock	Elvis Presley
38	7/08	7	1	4. (Let Me Be Your) Teddy Bear	Elvis Presley
62	12/16	6	1	5. April Love	Pat Boone
66	2/16	6	1	6. Young Love	Tab Hunter
80	8/19	5	1	7. Tammy	Debbie Reynolds
127	9/23	4	1	8. Honeycomb	Jimmie Rodgers
133	10/14	4	1	9. Wake Up Little Susie	The Everly Brothers
210	12/02	3	1	10. You Send Me	Sam Cooke
236	3/30	3	1	11. Butterfly	Andy Williams
248	2/09	3	1	12. Too Much	Elvis Presley
334	4/06	2	1	13. Round And Round	Perry Como
433	4/13	2	1	14. Butterfly	Charlie Gracie
562	10/21	1	1	15. Chances Are	Johnny Mathis
565	2/09	1	1	16. Don't Forbid Me	Pat Boone
566	2/09	1	1	17. Young Love	Sonny James
568	9/09	1	1	18. Diana	Paul Anka
586	3/30	1	1	19. Party Doll	Buddy Knox
607	9/23	1	1	20. That'll Be The Day	The Crickets
880	4/06	8	2	21. Little Darlin'	The Diamonds
894	6/17	4	2	22. So Rare	Jimmy Dorsey
896	6/17	4	2	23. Bye Bye Love	The Everly Brothers
924	1/19	3	2	24. Blueberry Hill	Fats Domino
	1/05	2	2	25. Love Me	Elvis Presley
	3/16	2	2	26. Teen-Age Crush	Tommy Sands
	6/03	1	2	27. A White Sport Coat (And A Pink Carnation)	Marty Robbins
	12/16	1	2	28. Raunchy	Bill Justis Orch.
	6/10	1	2	29. A Teenager's Romance	Ricky Nelson
	8/05	4	3	30. I'm Gonna Sit Right Down And Write Myself A Letter	Billy Williams
	12/16	1	3	31. Kisses Sweeter Than Wine	Jimmie Rodgers
	12/30	3	3	32. Peggy Sue	Buddy Holly
	5/13	3	3	33. School Day	Chuck Berry
	9/09	2	3	34. Whole Lot Of Shakin' Going On	Jerry Lee Lewis
	11/04	2	3	35. Silhouettes	The Rays
	7/29	1	3	36. Searchin'	The Coasters
	7/29	1	3	37. Old Cape Cod	Patti Page
	1/19	1	3	38. Moonlight Gambler	Frankie Laine
	1/12	1	3	39. Hey! Jealous Lover	Frank Sinatra
	4/06	1	3	40. Marianne	The Hilltoppers

TOP 40 HITS
1958

RANK	PK DATE	PK WKS	PK POS	TITLE	ARTIST
41	1/06	7	1	1. At The Hop	Danny & The Juniors
69	9/29	6	1	2. It's All In The Game	Tommy Edwards
76	6/09	6	1	3. The Purple People Eater	Sheb Wooley
90	5/12	5	1	4. All I Have To Do Is Dream	The Everly Brothers
93	3/17	5	1	5. Tequila	The Champs
98	2/10	5	1	6. Don't	Elvis Presley
105	8/18	5	1	7. Nel Blu Dipinto Di Blu (Volare)	Domenico Modugno
135	2/17	4	1	8. Sugartime	The McGuire Sisters
170	4/14	4	1	9. He's Got The Whole World (In His Hands)	Laurie London
195	12/22	4	1	10. The Chipmunk Song	The Chipmunks/David Seville
212	4/28	3	1	11. Witch Doctor	David Seville
218	12/01	3	1	12. To Know Him, Is To Love Him	The Teddy Bears
349	8/04	2	1	13. Poor Little Fool	Ricky Nelson
355	11/10	2	1	14. It's Only Make Believe	Conway Twitty
438	2/24	2	1	15. Get A Job	The Silhouettes
517	7/21	2	1	16. Hard Headed Woman	Elvis Presley
558	7/28	1	1	17. Patricia	Perez Prado & His Orch.
569	11/17	1	1	18. Tom Dooley	The Kingston Trio
571	3/24	1	1	19. Catch A Falling Star	Perry Como
572	4/21	1	1	20. Twilight Time	The Platters
576	8/25	1	1	21. Little Star	The Elegants
578	8/25	1	1	22. Bird Dog	The Everly Brothers
619	7/21	1	1	23. Yakety Yak	The Coasters
912	1/06	4	2	24. Great Balls Of Fire	Jerry Lee Lewis
959	3/10	3	2	25. 26 Miles (Santa Catalina)	The Four Preps
961	1/13	3	2	26. Stood Up	Ricky Nelson
974	3/17	3	2	27. Sweet Little Sixteen	Chuck Berry
	10/13	2	2	28. Rock-in Robin	Bobby Day
	3/31	2	2	29. Lollipop	The Chordettes
	1/06	1	2	30. All The Way	Frank Sinatra
	4/28	1	2	31. Wear My Ring Around Your Neck	Elvis Presley
	12/15	1	2	32. Problems	The Everly Brothers
	6/16	3	3	33. Secretly	Jimmie Rodgers
	10/20	3	3	34. Topsy II	Cozy Cole
	6/09	2	3	35. Big Man	The Four Preps
	2/10	2	3	36. Short Shorts	Royal Teens
	8/18	1	3	37. My True Love	Jack Scott
	8/04	1	3	38. Splish Splash	Bobby Darin
	3/24	1	3	39. Are You Sincere	Andy Williams
	3/10	5	4	40. A Wonderful Time Up There	Pat Boone

TOP 40 HITS
1959

RANK	PK DATE	PK WKS	PK POS	TITLE	ARTIST
14	10/05	9	1	1. Mack The Knife	Bobby Darin
65	6/01	6	1	2. The Battle Of New Orleans	Johnny Horton
103	3/09	5	1	3. Venus	Frankie Avalon
153	2/09	4	1	4. Stagger Lee	Lloyd Price
155	8/24	4	1	5. The Three Bells	The Browns
156	7/13	4	1	6. Lonely Boy	Paul Anka
188	4/13	4	1	7. Come Softly To Me	Fleetwoods
231	1/19	3	1	8. Smoke Gets In Your Eyes	The Platters
357	12/14	2	1	9. Heartaches By The Number	Guy Mitchell
389	9/21	2	1	10. Sleep Walk	Santo & Johnny
442	5/18	2	1	11. Kansas City	Wilbert Harrison
495	8/10	2	1	12. A Big Hunk O' Love	Elvis Presley
574	11/16	1	1	13. Mr. Blue	The Fleetwoods
629	12/28	1	1	14. Why	Frankie Avalon
715	5/11	1	1	15. The Happy Organ	Dave 'Baby' Cortez
939	10/05	3	2	16. Put Your Head On My Shoulder	Paul Anka
945	6/15	3	2	17. Personality	Lloyd Price
965	3/09	3	2	18. Charlie Brown	The Coasters
	2/23	2	2	19. Donna	Ritchie Valens
	2/09	2	2	20. 16 Candles	The Crests
	1/19	2	2	21. My Happiness	Connie Francis
	5/11	2	2	22. Sorry (I Ran All the Way Home)	The Impalas
	8/24	2	2	23. Sea Of Love	Phil Phillips with The Twilights
	6/08	1	2	24. Dream Lover	Bobby Darin
	11/30	1	2	25. Don't You Know	Della Reese
	8/17	1	2	26. There Goes My Baby	The Drifters
	2/02	1	2	27. The All American Boy	Bill Parsons
	4/27	1	2	28. (Now and Then There's) A Fool Such As I	Elvis Presley
	8/03	3	3	29. My Heart Is An Open Book	Carl Dobkins, Jr.
	4/13	2	3	30. Pink Shoe Laces	Dodie Stevens
	12/28	2	3	31. The Big Hurt	Miss Toni Fisher
	9/14	2	3	32. I'm Gonna Get Married	Lloyd Price
	7/20	2	3	33. Tiger	Fabian
	3/16	2	3	34. Alvin's Harmonica	The Chipmunks
	4/06	1	3	35. It's Just A Matter Of Time	Brook Benton
	8/24	1	3	36. Lavender-Blue	Sammy Turner
	9/21	3	4	37. ('Til) I Kissed You	The Everly Brothers
	7/13	3	4	38. Waterloo	Stonewall Jackson
	10/19	2	4	39. Teen Beat	Sandy Nelson
	6/01	2	4	40. Quiet Village	Martin Denny Orch.

TOP 40 HITS
1960

RANK	PK DATE	PK WKS	PK POS	TITLE	ARTIST
19	2/22	9	1	1. The Theme From "A Summer Place"	Percy Faith & His Orch.
75	11/28	6	1	2. Are You Lonesome To-night?	Elvis Presley
92	8/15	5	1	3. It's Now Or Never	Elvis Presley
111	5/23	5	1	4. Cathy's Clown	The Everly Brothers
158	4/25	4	1	5. Stuck On You	Elvis Presley
217	7/18	3	1	6. I'm Sorry	Brenda Lee
234	1/18	3	1	7. Running Bear	Johnny Preston
246	10/17	3	1	8. Save The Last Dance For Me	The Drifters
361	2/08	2	1	9. Teen Angel	Mark Dinning
362	9/26	2	1	10. My Heart Has A Mind Of Its Own	Connie Francis
379	1/04	2	1	11. El Paso	Marty Robbins
418	6/27	2	1	12. Everybody's Somebody's Fool	Connie Francis
197	9/19	1	1	13. The Twist	Chubby Checker
				re-entered at #1 in 1962	
671	8/08	1	1	14. Itsy Bitsy Teenie Weenie Yellow Polkadot Bikini	Brian Hyland
673	7/11	1	1	15. Alley-Oop	Hollywood Argyles
762	10/10	1	1	16. Mr. Custer	Larry Verne
813	10/24	1	1	17. I Want To Be Wanted	Brenda Lee
848	11/21	1	1	18. Stay	Maurice Williams & Zodiacs
864	11/14	1	1	19. Georgia On My Mind	Ray Charles
906	11/28	4	2	20. Last Date	Floyd Cramer
910	4/18	4	2	21. Greenfields	The Brothers Four
931	3/07	3	2	22. He'll Have To Go	Jim Reeves
	10/03	2	2	23. Chain Gang	Sam Cooke
	4/04	2	2	24. Puppy Love	Paul Anka
	2/29	1	2	25. Handy Man	Jimmy Jones
	8/29	1	2	26. Walk–Don't Run	The Ventures
	7/25	1	2	27. Only The Lonely (Know How I Feel)	Roy Orbison
	3/28	1	2	28. Wild One	Bobby Rydell
	11/14	1	2	29. Poetry In Motion	Johnny Tillotson
	5/23	3	3	30. Good Timin'	Jimmy Jones
	6/13	2	3	31. Burning Bridges	Jack Scott
	12/12	1	3	32. A Thousand Stars	Kathy Young with The Innocents
	5/02	1	3	33. Sixteen Reasons	Connie Stevens
	4/25	1	3	34. Sink The Bismarck	Johnny Horton
	1/11	1	3	35. Way Down Yonder In New Orleans	Freddie Cannon
	2/08	1	3	36. Where Or When	Dion & The Belmonts
	11/14	1	3	37. You Talk Too Much	Joe Jones
	5/09	2	4	38. Night	Jackie Wilson
	5/30	2	4	39. He'll Have To Stay	Jeanne Black
	7/04	2	4	40. Because They're Young	Duane Eddy & The Rebels

TOP 40 HITS
1961

RANK	PK DATE	PK WKS	PK POS	TITLE	ARTIST
42	7/10	7	1	1. Tossin' And Turnin'	Bobby Lewis
106	11/06	5	1	2. Big Bad John	Jimmy Dean
174	4/24	4	1	3. Runaway	Del Shannon
233	1/09	3	1	4. Wonderland By Night	Bert Kaempfert & His Orch.
264	2/27	3	1	5. Pony Time	Chubby Checker
274	12/18	3	1	6. The Lion Sleeps Tonight	The Tokens
282	4/03	3	1	7. Blue Moon	The Marcels
310	9/18	3	1	8. Take Good Care Of My Baby	Bobby Vee
390	2/13	2	1	9. Calcutta	Lawrence Welk & His Orch.
403	10/23	2	1	10. Runaround Sue	Dion
408	9/04	2	1	11. Michael	The Highwaymen
425	5/29	2	1	12. Travelin' Man	Ricky Nelson
444	6/26	2	1	13. Quarter To Three	U.S. Bonds
448	10/09	2	1	14. Hit The Road Jack	Ray Charles
450	3/20	2	1	15. Surrender	Elvis Presley
461	1/30	2	1	16. Will You Love Me Tomorrow	The Shirelles
674	5/22	1	1	17. Mother-In-Law	Ernie K-Doe
689	12/11	1	1	18. Please Mr. Postman	The Marvelettes
742	8/28	1	1	19. Wooden Heart	Joe Dowell
828	6/19	1	1	20. Moody River	Pat Boone
870	6/05	1	1	21. Running Scared	Roy Orbison
964	7/10	3	2	22. The Boll Weevil Song	Brook Benton
977	7/31	3	2	23. I Like It Like That, Part 1	Chris Kenner
	10/23	2	2	24. Bristol Stomp	The Dovells
	4/03	2	2	25. Apache	Jorgen Ingmann & His Guitar
	9/25	2	2	26. The Mountain's High	Dick & DeeDee
	1/23	1	2	27. Exodus	Ferrante & Teicher
	6/26	1	2	28. Raindrops	Dee Clark
	2/20	1	2	29. Shop Around	The Miracles
	12/25	1	2	30. Run To Him	Bobby Vee
	10/09	1	2	31. Crying	Roy Orbison
	5/29	1	2	32. Daddy's Home	Shep & The Limelites
	3/27	2	3	33. Dedicated To The One I Love	The Shirelles
	5/08	2	3	34. A Hundred Pounds Of Clay	Gene McDaniels
	12/04	2	3	35. Goodbye Cruel World	James Darren
	3/06	2	3	36. Wheels	The String-A-Longs
	8/07	2	3	37. Last Night	Mar-Keys
	11/13	2	3	38. Fool #1	Brenda Lee
	9/11	2	3	39. My True Story	The Jive Five
	3/20	1	3	40. Don't Worry	Marty Robbins

TOP 40 HITS
1962

RANK	PK DATE	PK WKS	PK POS		TITLE	ARTIST
97	6/02	5	1	1.	I Can't Stop Loving You	Ray Charles
104	11/17	5	1	2.	Big Girls Don't Cry	The 4 Seasons
117	9/15	5	1	3.	Sherry	The 4 Seasons
159	7/14	4	1	4.	Roses Are Red (My Love)	Bobby Vinton
223	1/27	3	1	5.	Peppermint Twist - Part I	Joey Dee & the Starliters
272	12/22	3	1	6.	Telstar	The Tornadoes
275	5/05	3	1	7.	Soldier Boy	The Shirelles
278	3/10	3	1	8.	Hey! Baby	Bruce Channel
280	2/17	3	1	9.	Duke Of Earl	Gene Chandler
197	1/13	2	1	10.	The Twist	Chubby Checker
					re-entry of #1 hit from 1960	
396	4/07	2	1	11.	Johnny Angel	Shelley Fabares
411	10/20	2	1	12.	Monster Mash	Bobby "Boris" Pickett
480	11/03	2	1	13.	He's A Rebel	The Crystals
485	8/11	2	1	14.	Breaking Up Is Hard To Do	Neil Sedaka
489	4/21	2	1	15.	Good Luck Charm	Elvis Presley
538	9/01	2	1	16.	Sheila	Tommy Roe
577	5/26	1	1	17.	Stranger On The Shore	Mr. Acker Bilk
626	7/07	1	1	18.	The Stripper	David Rose & His Orch.
741	8/25	1	1	19.	The Loco-Motion	Little Eva
840	3/31	1	1	20.	Don't Break The Heart That Loves You	Connie Francis
891	11/17	5	2	21.	Return To Sender	Elvis Presley
	12/22	2	2	22.	Limbo Rock	Chubby Checker
	5/05	2	2	23.	Mashed Potato Time	Dee Dee Sharp
	9/22	2	2	24.	Ramblin' Rose	Nat King Cole
	7/21	2	2	25.	The Wah Watusi	The Orlons
	2/03	1	2	26.	Can't Help Falling In Love	Elvis Presley
	2/24	1	2	27.	The Wanderer	Dion
	3/17	1	2	28.	Midnight In Moscow	Kenny Ball & his Jazzmen
	9/08	1	2	29.	You Don't Know Me	Ray Charles
	11/03	1	2	30.	Only Love Can Break A Heart	Gene Pitney
	12/01	4	3	31.	Bobby's Girl	Marcie Blane
	10/20	3	3	32.	Do You Love Me	The Contours
	11/10	2	3	33.	All Alone Am I	Brenda Lee
	6/23	2	3	34.	Palisades Park	Freddy Cannon
	7/28	2	3	35.	Sealed With A Kiss	Brian Hyland
	4/14	1	3	36.	Slow Twistin'	Chubby Checker (with Dee Dee Sharp)
	2/24	1	3	37.	Norman	Sue Thompson
	9/29	1	3	38.	Green Onions	Booker T. & The MG's
	6/16	1	3	39.	It Keeps Right On A-Hurtin'	Johnny Tillotson
	1/27	1	3	40.	I Know (You Don't Love Me No More)	Barbara George

LITTLE STAR

by
ARTHUR VENOSA
and
VITO PICONE

RECORDED BY THE ELEGANTS ON APT RECORDS

KEEL MUSIC PUBL. CO.

Sole Selling Agent:—KEYS-HANSEN, Inc.   •   119 West 57th Street   •   New York 19, N. Y.

WAKE UP, LITTLE SUSIE

By Boudleaux Bryant and Felice Bryant

RECORDED BY THE EVERLY BROTHERS FOR CADENCE RECORDS

Acuff-Rose PUBLICATIONS
2510 Franklin Road
NASHVILLE 4, TENNESSEE

TOP 40 HITS
1963

RANK	PK DATE	PK WKS	PK POS	TITLE	ARTIST
107	10/12	5	1	1. Sugar Shack	Jimmy Gilmer & The Fireball
175	3/30	4	1	2. He's So Fine	The Chiffons
177	12/07	4	1	3. Dominique	The Singing Nun
254	2/09	3	1	4. Hey Paula	Paul & Paula
255	8/31	3	1	5. My Boyfriend's Back	The Angels
277	9/21	3	1	6. Blue Velvet	Bobby Vinton
279	6/15	3	1	7. Sukiyaki	Kyu Sakamoto
283	4/27	3	1	8. I Will Follow Him	Little Peggy March
307	8/10	3	1	9. Fingertips - Pt 2	Little Stevie Wonder
309	3/02	3	1	10. Walk Like A Man	The 4 Seasons
402	1/12	2	1	11. Go Away Little Girl	Steve Lawrence
484	11/23	2	1	12. I'm Leaving It Up To You	Dale & Grace
490	7/20	2	1	13. Surf City	Jan & Dean
491	6/01	2	1	14. It's My Party	Lesley Gore
492	1/26	2	1	15. Walk Right In	The Rooftop Singers
496	7/06	2	1	16. Easier Said Than Done	The Essex
539	5/18	2	1	17. If You Wanna Be Happy	Jimmy Soul
746	8/03	1	1	18. So Much In Love	The Tymes
747	11/16	1	1	19. Deep Purple	Nino Tempo & April Stevens
839	3/23	1	1	20. Our Day Will Come	Ruby & The Romantics
889	12/14	6	2	21. Louie Louie	The Kingsmen
917	4/13	4	2	22. Can't Get Used To Losing You	Andy Williams
989	2/23	3	2	23. Ruby Baby	Dion
991	10/12	3	2	24. Be My Baby	The Ronettes
994	8/24	3	2	25. Hello Mudduh, Hello Fadduh! (A Letter From Camp)	Allan Sherman
	9/28	2	2	26. Sally, Go 'Round The Roses	The Jaynetts
	8/10	1	2	27. Wipe Out	The Surfaris
	8/17	1	2	28. Blowin' In The Wind	Peter, Paul & Mary
	11/23	1	2	29. Washington Square	The Village Stompers
	3/23	1	2	30. The End Of The World	Skeeter Davis
	5/11	1	2	31. Puff (The Magic Dragon)	Peter, Paul & Mary
	9/07	3	3	32. If I Had A Hammer	Trini Lopez
	3/16	2	3	33. You're The Reason I'm Living	Bobby Darin
	2/02	2	3	34. The Night Has A Thousand Eyes	Bobby Vee
	12/07	2	3	35. Everybody	Tommy Roe
	8/10	2	3	36. (You're the) Devil In Disguise	Elvis Presley
	6/22	2	3	37. Hello Stranger	Barbara Lewis
	3/09	1	3	38. Rhythm Of The Rain	The Cascades
	5/25	1	3	39. Surfin' U.S.A.	Beach Boys
	6/01	1	3	40. I Love You Because	Al Martino

TOP 40 HITS
1964

RANK	PK DATE	PK WKS	PK POS	TITLE	ARTIST
45	2/01	7	1	1. I Want To Hold Your Hand	The Beatles
118	4/04	5	1	2. Can't Buy Me Love	The Beatles
178	1/04	4	1	3. There! I've Said It Again	Bobby Vinton
190	10/31	4	1	4. Baby Love	The Supremes
266	9/26	3	1	5. Oh, Pretty Woman	Roy Orbison
287	9/05	3	1	6. The House Of The Rising Sun	The Animals
312	6/06	3	1	7. Chapel Of Love	The Dixie Cups
315	12/26	3	1	8. I Feel Fine	The Beatles
351	3/21	2	1	9. She Loves You	The Beatles
393	7/04	2	1	10. I Get Around	The Beach Boys
400	12/19	2	1	11. Come See About Me	The Supremes
401	8/22	2	1	12. Where Did Our Love Go	The Supremes
407	10/17	2	1	13. Do Wah Diddy Diddy	Manfred Mann
437	5/16	2	1	14. My Guy	Mary Wells
446	8/01	2	1	15. A Hard Day's Night	The Beatles
493	7/18	2	1	16. Rag Doll	The 4 Seasons
564	5/09	1	1	17. Hello, Dolly!	Louis Armstrong
625	12/12	1	1	18. Mr. Lonely	Bobby Vinton
670	8/15	1	1	19. Everybody Loves Somebody	Dean Martin
678	6/27	1	1	20. A World Without Love	Peter & Gordon
765	12/05	1	1	21. Ringo	Lorne Greene
834	5/30	1	1	22. Love Me Do	The Beatles
865	11/28	1	1	23. Leader Of The Pack	The Shangri-Las
916	4/04	4	2	24. Twist And Shout	The Beatles
998	2/01	3	2	25. You Don't Own Me	Lesley Gore
	10/17	2	2	26. Dancing In The Street	Martha & The Vandellas
	9/19	2	2	27. Bread And Butter	The Newbeats
	7/11	2	2	28. Memphis	Johnny Rivers
	11/07	1	2	29. Last Kiss	J. Frank Wilson & The Cavaliers
	12/12	1	2	30. She's Not There	The Zombies
	7/04	1	2	31. My Boy Lollipop	Millie Small
	5/09	1	2	32. Do You Want To Know A Secret	The Beatles
	2/22	3	3	33. Dawn (Go Away)	The Four Seasons
	4/11	2	3	34. Suspicion	Terry Stafford
	3/14	2	3	35. Please Please Me	The Beatles
	1/11	2	3	36. Popsicles And Icicles	The Murmaids
	2/01	2	3	37. Out Of Limits	The Marketts
	11/21	2	3	38. Come A Little Bit Closer	Jay & The Americans
	6/13	1	3	39. Love Me With All Your Heart (Cuando Calienta El Sol)	Ray Charles Singers
	8/01	1	3	40. The Little Old Lady (From Pasadena)	Jan & Dean

TOP 40 HITS
1965

RANK	PK DATE	PK WKS	PK POS	TITLE	ARTIST
176	7/10	4	1	1. (I Can't Get No) Satisfaction	The Rolling Stones
196	10/09	4	1	2. Yesterday	The Beatles
281	12/04	3	1	3. Turn! Turn! Turn! (To Everything There Is A Season)	The Byrds
314	5/01	3	1	4. Mrs. Brown You've Got A Lovely Daughter	Herman's Hermits
316	8/14	3	1	5. I Got You Babe	Sonny & Cher
322	9/04	3	1	6. Help!	The Beatles
365	6/19	2	1	7. I Can't Help Myself	Four Tops
391	2/06	2	1	8. You've Lost That Lovin' Feelin'	The Righteous Brothers
395	1/23	2	1	9. Downtown	Petula Clark
409	2/20	2	1	10. This Diamond Ring	Gary Lewis & The Playboys
451	3/27	2	1	11. Stop! In The Name Of Love	The Supremes
488	5/29	2	1	12. Help Me, Rhonda	The Beach Boys
540	11/06	2	1	13. Get Off Of My Cloud	The Rolling Stones
546	11/20	2	1	14. I Hear A Symphony	The Supremes
548	4/10	2	1	15. I'm Telling You Now	Freddie & The Dreamers
554	3/13	2	1	16. Eight Days A Week	The Beatles
677	3/06	1	1	17. My Girl	The Temptations
761	10/02	1	1	18. Hang On Sloopy	The McCoys
764	6/26	1	1	19. Mr. Tambourine Man	The Byrds
767	9/25	1	1	20. Eve Of Destruction	Barry McGuire
836	12/25	1	1	21. Over And Over	The Dave Clark Five
842	5/22	1	1	22. Ticket To Ride	The Beatles
843	8/07	1	1	23. I'm Henry VIII, I Am	Herman's Hermits
866	4/24	1	1	24. Game Of Love	Wayne Fontana/Mindbenders
867	6/12	1	1	25. Back In My Arms Again	The Supremes
988	10/30	3	2	26. A Lover's Concerto	The Toys
	6/05	2	2	27. Wooly Bully	Sam The Sham/Pharaohs
	3/27	2	2	28. Can't You Hear My Heartbeat	Herman's Hermits
	9/04	2	2	29. Like A Rolling Stone	Bob Dylan
	10/16	2	2	30. Treat Her Right	Roy Head & The Traits
	5/08	2	2	31. Count Me In	Gary Lewis/The Playboys
	11/20	1	2	32. 1-2-3	Len Barry
	8/21	1	2	33. Save Your Heart For Me	Gary Lewis/The Playboys
	12/18	3	3	34. I Got You (I Feel Good)	James Brown
	3/20	2	3	35. The Birds And The Bees	Jewel Akens
	1/16	2	3	36. Love Potion Number Nine	The Searchers
	1/30	2	3	37. The Name Game	Shirley Ellis
	7/31	2	3	38. What's New Pussycat?	Tom Jones
	8/28	2	3	39. California Girls	The Beach Boys
	12/11	1	3	40. Let's Hang On!	The 4 Seasons

TOP 40 HITS
1966

RANK	PK DATE	PK WKS	PK POS	TITLE	ARTIST
46	12/31	7	1	1. I'm A Believer	The Monkees
116	3/05	5	1	2. The Ballad Of The Green Berets	SSgt Barry Sadler
238	12/03	3	1	3. Winchester Cathedral	New Vaudeville Band
284	4/09	3	1	4. (You're My) Soul And Inspiration	The Righteous Brothers
285	5/07	3	1	5. Monday, Monday	The Mama's & The Papa's
313	1/08	3	1	6. We Can Work It Out	The Beatles
317	8/13	3	1	7. Summer In The City	The Lovin' Spoonful
321	9/24	3	1	8. Cherish	The Association
449	9/10	2	1	9. You Can't Hurry Love	The Supremes
452	7/30	2	1	10. Wild Thing	The Troggs
483	10/15	2	1	11. Reach Out I'll Be There	Four Tops
499	6/11	2	1	12. Paint It, Black	The Rolling Stones
542	5/28	2	1	13. When A Man Loves A Woman	Percy Sledge
543	11/19	2	1	14. You Keep Me Hangin' On	The Supremes
544	7/16	2	1	15. Hanky Panky	Tommy James & The Shondells
547	2/05	2	1	16. My Love	Petula Clark
549	1/01	2	1	17. The Sounds Of Silence	Simon & Garfunkel
553	6/25	2	1	18. Paperback Writer	The Beatles
630	10/29	1	1	19. 96 Tears	? & The Mysterians
631	11/05	1	1	20. Last Train To Clarksville	The Monkees
745	11/12	1	1	21. Poor Side Of Town	Johnny Rivers
748	2/26	1	1	22. These Boots Are Made For Walkin'	Nancy Sinatra
749	12/10	1	1	23. Good Vibrations	The Beach Boys
750	4/30	1	1	24. Good Lovin'	The Young Rascals
757	7/02	1	1	25. Strangers In The Night	Frank Sinatra
763	9/03	1	1	26. Sunshine Superman	Donovan
837	2/19	1	1	27. Lightnin' Strikes	Lou Christie
915	12/31	4	2	28. Snoopy Vs. The Red Baron	The Royal Guardsmen
978	12/10	3	2	29. Mellow Yellow	Donovan
992	3/19	3	2	30. 19th Nervous Breakdown	The Rolling Stones
	8/06	2	2	31. Lil' Red Riding Hood	Sam The Sham/Pharaohs
	4/09	2	2	32. Daydream	The Lovin' Spoonful
	8/20	2	2	33. Sunny	Bobby Hebb
	6/11	2	2	34. Did You Ever Have To Make Up Your Mind?	The Lovin' Spoonful
	5/28	2	2	35. A Groovy Kind Of Love	The Mindbenders
	1/29	2	2	36. Barbara Ann	The Beach Boys with Dean Torrence
	7/09	1	2	37. Red Rubber Ball	The Cyrkle
	4/23	1	2	38. Bang Bang (My Baby Shot Me Down)	Cher
	9/17	1	2	39. Yellow Submarine	The Beatles
	5/21	1	2	40. Rainy Day Women #12 & 35	Bob Dylan

TOP 40 HITS
1967

RANK	PK DATE	PK WKS	PK POS	TITLE	ARTIST
110	10/21	5	1	1. To Sir With Love	Lulu
161	12/02	4	1	2. Daydream Believer	The Monkees
172	7/01	4	1	3. Windy	The Association
173	8/26	4	1	4. Ode To Billie Joe	Bobbie Gentry
179	4/15	4	1	5. Somethin' Stupid	Nancy Sinatra & Frank Sinatra
180	5/20	4	1	6. Groovin'	The Young Rascals
186	9/23	4	1	7. The Letter	The Box Tops
245	7/29	3	1	8. Light My Fire	The Doors
253	3/25	3	1	9. Happy Together	The Turtles
286	12/30	3	1	10. Hello Goodbye	The Beatles
494	6/03	2	1	11. Respect	Aretha Franklin
497	2/18	2	1	12. Kind Of A Drag	The Buckinghams
624	11/25	1	1	13. Incense And Peppermints	Strawberry Alarm Clock
766	3/11	1	1	14. Love Is Here And Now You're Gone	The Supremes
768	3/04	1	1	15. Ruby Tuesday	The Rolling Stones
769	8/19	1	1	16. All You Need Is Love	The Beatles
841	5/13	1	1	17. The Happening	The Supremes
869	3/18	1	1	18. Penny Lane	The Beatles
954	12/16	3	2	19. I Heard It Through The Grapevine	Gladys Knight & The Pips
966	11/04	3	2	20. Soul Man	Sam & Dave
993	3/25	3	2	21. Dedicated To The One I Love	The Mamas & The Papas
	7/08	2	2	22. Little Bit O'Soul	The Music Explosion
	12/02	2	2	23. The Rain, The Park & Other Things	The Cowsills
	2/04	2	2	24. Georgy Girl	The Seekers
	10/07	2	2	25. Never My Love	The Association
	7/29	2	2	26. I Was Made To Love Her	Stevie Wonder
	9/09	2	2	27. Reflections	Diana Ross & The Supremes
	7/22	1	2	28. Can't Take My Eyes Off You	Frankie Valli
	1/28	1	2	29. Tell It Like It Is	Aaron Neville
	5/13	1	2	30. Sweet Soul Music	Arthur Conley
	4/29	1	2	31. A Little Bit Me, A Little Bit You	The Monkees
	9/09	3	3	32. Come Back When You Grow Up	Bobby Vee/The Strangers
	5/27	3	3	33. I Got Rhythm	The Happenings
	11/04	2	3	34. It Must Be Him	Vikki Carr
	8/19	2	3	35. Pleasant Valley Sunday	The Monkees
	3/11	2	3	36. Baby I Need Your Lovin'	Johnny Rivers
	6/17	2	3	37. She'd Rather Be With Me	The Turtles
	4/15	1	3	38. This Is My Song	Petula Clark
	5/27	4	4	39. Release Me (And Let Me Love Again)	Engelbert Humperdinck
	7/01	4	4	40. San Francisco (Be Sure To Wear Flowers In Your Hair)	Scott McKenzie

TOP 40 HITS
1968

RANK	PK DATE	PK WKS	PK POS	TITLE	ARTIST
17	9/28	9	1	1. Hey Jude	The Beatles
48	12/14	7	1	2. I Heard It Through The Grapevine	Marvin Gaye
101	2/10	5	1	3. Love Is Blue	Paul Mauriat & His Orch.
108	4/13	5	1	4. Honey	Bobby Goldsboro
113	8/17	5	1	5. People Got To Be Free	The Rascals
145	3/16	4	1	6. (Sittin' On) The Dock Of The Bay	Otis Redding
189	6/22	4	1	7. This Guy's In Love With You	Herb Alpert
308	6/01	3	1	8. Mrs. Robinson	Simon & Garfunkel
347	11/30	2	1	9. Love Child	Diana Ross & The Supremes
398	5/18	2	1	10. Tighten Up	Archie Bell & The Drells
410	8/03	2	1	11. Hello, I Love You	The Doors
435	1/20	2	1	12. Judy In Disguise (With Glasses)	John Fred & His Playboy Band
498	7/20	2	1	13. Grazing In The Grass	Hugh Masekela
632	9/21	1	1	14. Harper Valley P.T.A.	Jeannie C. Riley
752	2/03	1	1	15. Green Tambourine	The Lemon Pipers
918	2/24	4	2	16. (Theme From) Valley Of The Dolls	Dionne Warwick
962	4/06	3	2	17. Young Girl	Union Gap feat. Gary Puckett
970	11/02	3	2	18. Those Were The Days	Mary Hopkin
985	6/29	3	2	19. The Horse	Cliff Nobles & Co.
986	8/24	3	2	20. Born To Be Wild	Steppenwolf
	12/28	2	2	21. For Once In My Life	Stevie Wonder
	1/20	2	2	22. Chain Of Fools	Aretha Franklin
	4/27	2	2	23. Cry Like A Baby	The Box Tops
	8/03	2	2	24. Classical Gas	Mason Williams
	7/20	2	2	25. Lady Willpower	Gary Puckett/Union Gap
	10/26	1	2	26. Little Green Apples	O.C. Smith
	6/01	1	2	27. The Good, The Bad And The Ugly	Hugo Montenegro Orch.
	10/19	1	2	28. Fire	Crazy World Of Arthur Brown
	6/22	1	2	29. MacArthur Park	Richard Harris
	7/27	3	3	30. Stoned Soul Picnic	The 5th Dimension
	2/10	3	3	31. Spooky	Classics IV
	7/06	3	3	32. Jumpin' Jack Flash	The Rolling Stones
	8/31	3	3	33. Light My Fire	Jose Feliciano
	5/25	2	3	34. A Beautiful Morning	The Rascals
	3/30	2	3	35. Valleri	The Monkees
	11/30	1	3	36. Magic Carpet Ride	Steppenwolf
	6/15	1	3	37. Mony Mony	Tommy James & The Shondells
	3/09	4	4	38. Simon Says	1910 Fruitgum Co.
	1/13	3	4	39. Woman, Woman	Union Gap feat. Gary Puckett
	2/17	3	4	40. I Wish It Would Rain	The Temptations

TOP 40 HITS
1969

RANK	PK DATE	PK WKS	PK POS	TITLE	ARTIST
71	4/12	6	1	1. Aquarius/Let The Sunshine In (The Flesh Failures)	The 5th Dimension
79	7/12	6	1	2. In The Year 2525 (Exordium & Terminus)	Zager & Evans
115	5/24	5	1	3. Get Back	The Beatles with Billy Preston
136	9/20	4	1	4. Sugar, Sugar	The Archies
146	8/23	4	1	5. Honky Tonk Women	The Rolling Stones
168	2/15	4	1	6. Everyday People	Sly & The Family Stone
171	3/15	4	1	7. Dizzy	Tommy Roe
268	11/08	3	1	8. Wedding Bell Blues	The 5th Dimension
346	10/18	2	1	9. I Can't Get Next To You	The Temptations
348	2/01	2	1	10. Crimson And Clover	Tommy James & The Shondells
434	12/06	2	1	11. Na Na Hey Hey Kiss Him Goodbye	Steam
445	6/28	2	1	12. Love Theme From Romeo & Juliet	Henry Mancini & His Orch.
587	12/20	1	1	13. Leaving On A Jet Plane	Peter, Paul & Mary
613	11/29	1	1	14. Come Together	The Beatles
617	12/27	1	1	15. Someday We'll Be Together	Diana Ross & The Supremes
814	11/01	1	1	16. Suspicious Minds	Elvis Presley
956	7/26	3	2	17. Crystal Blue Persuasion	Tommy James & The Shondells
971	3/08	3	2	18. Proud Mary	Creedence Clearwater Revival
973	7/05	3	2	19. Spinning Wheel	Blood, Sweat & Tears
975	8/23	3	2	20. A Boy Named Sue	Johnny Cash
990	4/12	3	2	21. You've Made Me So Very Happy	Blood, Sweat & Tears
	5/10	2	2	22. Hair	The Cowsills
	1/11	2	2	23. I'm Gonna Make You Love Me	Supremes & Temptations
	10/18	2	2	24. Hot Fun In The Summertime	Sly & The Family Stone
	10/04	2	2	25. Jean	Oliver
	5/31	2	2	26. Love (Can Make You Happy)	Mercy
	9/27	1	2	27. Green River	Creedence Clearwater Revival
	11/22	1	2	28. Take A Letter Maria	R.B. Greaves
	5/03	1	2	29. It's Your Thing	The Isley Brothers
	11/29	1	2	30. And When I Die	Blood, Sweat & Tears
	6/28	1	2	31. Bad Moon Rising	Creedence Clearwater Revival
	3/29	1	2	32. Traces	Classics IV Featuring Dennis Yost
	2/22	3	3	33. Build Me Up Buttercup	The Foundations
	10/04	2	3	34. Little Woman	Bobby Sherman
	2/01	2	3	35. Worst That Could Happen	Brooklyn Bridge
	3/29	2	3	36. Time Of The Season	The Zombies
	7/12	2	3	37. Good Morning Starshine	Oliver
	11/15	2	3	38. Something	The Beatles
	1/11	1	3	39. Wichita Lineman	Glen Campbell
	12/20	1	3	40. Down On The Corner	Creedence Clearwater Revival

TOP 40 HITS
1970

RANK	PK DATE	PK WKS	PK POS	TITLE	ARTIST
77	2/28	6	1	1. Bridge Over Troubled Water	Simon & Garfunkel
94	10/17	5	1	2. I'll Be There	The Jackson 5
129	1/03	4	1	3. Raindrops Keep Fallin' On My Head	B.J. Thomas
144	7/25	4	1	4. (They Long To Be) Close To You	Carpenters
160	12/26	4	1	5. My Sweet Lord	George Harrison
221	11/21	3	1	6. I Think I Love You	The Partridge Family
252	9/19	3	1	7. Ain't No Mountain High Enough	Diana Ross
267	5/09	3	1	8. American Woman	The Guess Who
273	8/29	3	1	9. War	Edwin Starr
352	4/11	2	1	10. Let It Be	The Beatles
363	12/12	2	1	11. The Tears Of A Clown	Smokey Robinson & Miracles
397	7/11	2	1	12. Mama Told Me (Not To Come)	Three Dog Night
404	4/25	2	1	13. ABC	The Jackson 5
405	6/27	2	1	14. The Love You Save	The Jackson 5
486	2/14	2	1	15. Thank You (Falettinme Be Mice Elf Agin)	Sly & The Family Stone
528	5/30	2	1	16. Everything Is Beautiful	Ray Stevens
545	6/13	2	1	17. The Long And Winding Road	The Beatles
593	8/22	1	1	18. Make It With You	Bread
611	1/31	1	1	19. I Want You Back	The Jackson 5
628	2/07	1	1	20. Venus	The Shocking Blue
717	10/10	1	1	21. Cracklin' Rosie	Neil Diamond
911	10/31	4	2	22. We've Only Just Begun	Carpenters
	12/26	2	2	23. One Less Bell To Answer	The 5th Dimension
	6/06	2	2	24. Which Way You Goin' Billy?	The Poppy Family/Susan Jacks
	3/07	2	2	25. Travelin' Band	Creedence Clearwater Revival
	10/03	1	2	26. Lookin' Out My Back Door	Creedence Clearwater Revival
	2/21	1	2	27. Hey There Lonely Girl	Eddie Holman
	3/21	1	2	28. The Rapper	The Jaggerz
	5/23	1	2	29. Vehicle	The Ides Of March
	6/27	3	3	30. Ball Of Confusion (That's What The World Is Today)	The Temptations
	10/31	3	3	31. Fire And Rain	James Taylor
	4/18	3	3	32. Spirit In The Sky	Norman Greenbaum
	3/28	3	3	33. Instant Karma (We All Shine On)	John Ono Lennon
	12/05	2	3	34. Gypsy Woman	Brian Hyland
	10/03	2	3	35. Candida	Dawn
	10/17	2	3	36. Green-Eyed Lady	Sugarloaf
	8/08	2	3	37. Signed, Sealed, Delivered I'm Yours	Stevie Wonder
	5/30	2	3	38. Love On A Two-Way Street	The Moments
	7/25	1	3	39. Band Of Gold	Freda Payne
	8/22	1	3	40. Spill The Wine	Eric Burdon & War

TOP 40 HITS
1971

RANK	PK DATE	PK WKS	PK POS	TITLE	ARTIST
74	4/17	6	1	1. Joy To The World	Three Dog Night
96	10/02	5	1	2. Maggie May	Rod Stewart
102	6/19	5	1	3. It's Too Late	Carole King
114	2/13	5	1	4. One Bad Apple	The Osmonds
157	8/07	4	1	5. How Can You Mend A Broken Heart	The Bee Gees
222	1/23	3	1	6. Knock Three Times	Dawn
237	12/25	3	1	7. Brand New Key	Melanie
250	9/11	3	1	8. Go Away Little Girl	Donny Osmond
251	12/04	3	1	9. Family Affair	Sly & The Family Stone
386	11/06	2	1	10. Gypsys, Tramps & Thieves	Cher
394	4/03	2	1	11. Just My Imagination (Running Away With Me)	The Temptations
406	11/20	2	1	12. Theme From Shaft	Isaac Hayes
443	3/20	2	1	13. Me And Bobby McGee	Janis Joplin
447	5/29	2	1	14. Brown Sugar	The Rolling Stones
615	7/24	1	1	15. Indian Reservation (The Lament Of The Cherokee Reservation Indian)	Raiders
669	6/12	1	1	16. Want Ads	The Honey Cone
675	7/31	1	1	17. You've Got A Friend	James Taylor
751	9/04	1	1	18. Uncle Albert/Admiral Halsey	Paul & Linda McCartney
963	4/10	3	2	19. What's Going On	Marvin Gaye
976	5/08	3	2	20. Never Can Say Goodbye	The Jackson 5
	8/14	2	2	21. Mr. Big Stuff	Jean Knight
	10/16	2	2	22. Superstar	Carpenters
	6/19	2	2	23. Rainy Days And Mondays	Carpenters
	9/11	2	2	24. Spanish Harlem	Aretha Franklin
	2/27	2	2	25. Mama's Pearl	The Jackson 5
	8/28	1	2	26. Take Me Home, Country Roads	John Denver With Fat City
	3/20	1	2	27. She's A Lady	Tom Jones
	5/01	1	2	28. Put Your Hand In The Hand	Ocean
	10/16	3	3	29. Yo-Yo	The Osmonds
	12/11	2	3	30. Have You Seen Her	Chi-Lites
	7/03	2	3	31. Treat Her Like A Lady	Cornelius Brothers & Sister Rose
	3/13	2	3	32. For All We Know	Carpenters
	2/13	2	3	33. Rose Garden	Lynn Anderson
	9/04	2	3	34. Smiling Faces Sometimes	The Undisputed Truth
	9/18	2	3	35. Ain't No Sunshine	Bill Withers
	11/13	2	3	36. Imagine	John Lennon Plastic Ono Band
	11/27	2	3	37. Baby I'm-A Want You	Bread
	10/02	1	3	38. The Night They Drove Old Dixie Down	Joan Baez
	1/30	1	3	39. Lonely Days	Bee Gees
	8/28	1	3	40. Signs	Five Man Electrical Band

TOP 40 HITS
1972

RANK	PK DATE	PK WKS	PK POS	TITLE	ARTIST
72	4/15	6	1	1. The First Time Ever I Saw Your Face	Roberta Flack
73	7/29	6	1	2. Alone Again (Naturally)	Gilbert O'Sullivan
143	1/15	4	1	3. American Pie - Parts I & II	Don McLean
169	2/19	4	1	4. Without You	Nilsson
183	11/04	4	1	5. I Can See Clearly Now	Johnny Nash
239	3/25	3	1	6. A Horse With No Name	America
249	9/23	3	1	7. Baby Don't Get Hooked On Me	Mac Davis
265	12/16	3	1	8. Me And Mrs. Jones	Billy Paul
291	6/10	3	1	9. The Candy Man	Sammy Davis, Jr.
296	7/08	3	1	10. Lean On Me	Bill Withers
535	10/21	2	1	11. My Ding-A-Ling	Chuck Berry
591	8/26	1	1	12. Brandy (You're A Fine Girl)	Looking Glass
618	2/12	1	1	13. Let's Stay Together	Al Green
656	12/09	1	1	14. I Am Woman	Helen Reddy
665	6/03	1	1	15. I'll Take You There	The Staple Singers
672	3/18	1	1	16. Heart Of Gold	Neil Young
718	5/27	1	1	17. Oh Girl	Chi-Lites
754	10/14	1	1	18. Ben	Michael Jackson
827	12/02	1	1	19. Papa Was A Rollin' Stone	The Temptations
830	7/01	1	1	20. Song Sung Blue	Neil Diamond
868	9/16	1	1	21. Black & White	Three Dog Night
	5/06	2	2	22. I Gotcha	Joe Tex
	9/02	2	2	23. Long Cool Woman (In A Black Dress)	The Hollies
	7/15	2	2	24. Too Late To Turn Back Now	Cornelius Brothers & Sister Rose
	4/22	2	2	25. Rockin' Robin	Michael Jackson
	11/04	2	2	26. Nights In White Satin	The Moody Blues
	12/30	2	2	27. Clair	Gilbert O'Sullivan
	2/26	2	2	28. Hurting Each Other	Carpenters
	11/18	2	2	29. I'd Love You To Want Me	Lobo
	10/14	2	2	30. Use Me	Bill Withers
	7/08	1	2	31. Outa-Space	Billy Preston
	10/28	1	2	32. Burning Love	Elvis Presley
	3/11	3	3	33. The Lion Sleeps Tonight	Robert John
	8/05	2	3	34. (If Loving You Is Wrong) I Don't Want To Be Right	Luther Ingram
	2/26	2	3	35. Precious And Few	Climax
	12/23	2	3	36. You Ought To Be With Me	Al Green
	9/02	2	3	37. I'm Still In Love With You	Al Green
	12/09	2	3	38. If You Don't Know Me By Now	Harold Melvin & The Bluenotes
	11/18	2	3	39. I'll Be Around	The Spinners
	9/23	2	3	40. Saturday In The Park	Chicago

TOP 40 HITS
1973

RANK	PK DATE	PK WKS	PK POS	TITLE	ARTIST
112	2/24	5	1	1. Killing Me Softly With His Song	Roberta Flack
142	4/21	4	1	2. Tie A Yellow Ribbon Round The Ole Oak Tree	Dawn Featuring Tony Orlando
167	6/02	4	1	3. My Love	Paul McCartney & Wings
224	1/06	3	1	4. You're So Vain	Carly Simon
247	2/03	3	1	5. Crocodile Rock	Elton John
337	9/08	2	1	6. Let's Get It On	Marvin Gaye
359	11/10	2	1	7. Keep On Truckin' (Part 1)	Eddie Kendricks
414	7/21	2	1	8. Bad, Bad Leroy Brown	Jim Croce
416	12/01	2	1	9. Top Of The World	Carpenters
417	10/27	2	1	10. Midnight Train To Georgia	Gladys Knight & The Pips
424	8/25	2	1	11. Brother Louie	Stories
427	7/07	2	1	12. Will It Go Round In Circles	Billy Preston
428	10/06	2	1	13. Half-Breed	Cher
468	4/07	2	1	14. The Night The Lights Went Out In Georgia	Vicki Lawrence
482	12/29	2	1	15. Time In A Bottle	Jim Croce
500	12/15	2	1	16. The Most Beautiful Girl	Charlie Rich
537	8/04	2	1	17. The Morning After	Maureen McGovern
640	8/18	1	1	18. Touch Me In The Morning	Diana Ross
661	9/15	1	1	19. Delta Dawn	Helen Reddy
709	5/26	1	1	20. Frankenstein	The Edgar Winter Group
730	5/19	1	1	21. You Are The Sunshine Of My Life	Stevie Wonder
733	10/20	1	1	22. Angie	The Rolling Stones
760	6/30	1	1	23. Give Me Love - (Give Me Peace On Earth)	George Harrison
809	9/29	1	1	24. We're An American Band	Grand Funk
811	1/27	1	1	25. Superstition	Stevie Wonder
815	3/24	1	1	26. Love Train	O'Jays
825	11/24	1	1	27. Photograph	Ringo Starr
920	2/24	4	2	28. Dueling Banjos	Eric Weissberg & Steve Mandel
969	12/08	3	2	29. Goodbye Yellow Brick Road	Elton John
972	8/11	3	2	30. Live And Let Die	Wings
	6/16	2	2	31. Playground In My Mind	Clint Holmes
	7/07	2	2	32. Kodachrome	Paul Simon
	4/07	2	2	33. Neither One Of Us (Wants To Be The First To Say Goodbye)	Gladys Knight & The Pips
	4/28	2	2	34. The Cisco Kid	War
	10/06	1	2	35. Loves Me Like A Rock	Paul Simon
	6/02	1	2	36. Daniel	Elton John
	10/13	1	2	37. Ramblin Man	The Allman Brothers Band
	7/28	1	2	38. Yesterday Once More	Carpenters
	3/31	1	2	39. Also Sprach Zarathustra (2001)	Deodato
	5/05	3	3	40. Little Willy	The Sweet

TOP 40 HITS
1974

RANK	PK DATE	PK WKS	PK POS	TITLE	ARTIST
241	2/02	3	1	1. The Way We Were	Barbra Streisand
258	3/02	3	1	2. Seasons In The Sun	Terry Jacks
276	5/18	3	1	3. The Streak	Ray Stevens
323	8/24	3	1	4. (You're) Having My Baby	Paul Anka with Odia Coates
440	12/07	2	1	5. Kung Fu Fighting	Carl Douglas
479	6/15	2	1	6. Billy, Don't Be A Hero	Bo Donaldson & The Heywoods
487	7/27	2	1	7. Annie's Song	John Denver
511	5/04	2	1	8. The Loco-Motion	Grand Funk
516	4/20	2	1	9. TSOP (The Sound Of Philadelphia)	MFSB with The Three Degrees
533	11/23	2	1	10. I Can Help	Billy Swan
551	10/05	2	1	11. I Honestly Love You	Olivia Newton-John
552	7/13	2	1	12. Rock Your Baby	George McCrae
612	4/13	1	1	13. Bennie And The Jets	Elton John
642	1/12	1	1	14. The Joker	Steve Miller Band
652	10/26	1	1	15. Then Came You	Dionne Warwicke & Spinners
683	2/09	1	1	16. Love's Theme	Love Unlimited Orchestra
684	1/19	1	1	17. Show And Tell	Al Wilson
710	11/02	1	1	18. You Haven't Done Nothin	Stevie Wonder
713	10/19	1	1	19. Nothing From Nothing	Billy Preston
716	4/06	1	1	20. Hooked On A Feeling	Blue Swede
727	3/30	1	1	21. Sunshine On My Shoulders	John Denver
728	6/08	1	1	22. Band On The Run	Paul McCartney & Wings
743	1/26	1	1	23. You're Sixteen	Ringo Starr
753	6/29	1	1	24. Sundown	Gordon Lightfoot
805	9/28	1	1	25. Rock Me Gently	Andy Kim
808	12/28	1	1	26. Angie Baby	Helen Reddy
812	8/10	1	1	27. Feel Like Makin' Love	Roberta Flack
819	12/21	1	1	28. Cat's In The Cradle	Harry Chapin
826	3/23	1	1	29. Dark Lady	Cher
832	8/17	1	1	30. The Night Chicago Died	Paper Lace
856	11/09	1	1	31. You Ain't Seen Nothing Yet	Bachman-Turner Overdrive
861	7/06	1	1	32. Rock The Boat	The Hues Corporation
863	9/14	1	1	33. I Shot The Sheriff	Eric Clapton
875	9/21	1	1	34. Can't Get Enough Of Your Love, Babe	Barry White
876	11/16	1	1	35. Whatever Gets You Thru The Night	John Lennon/Plastic Ono Band
	5/18	2	2	36. Dancing Machine	The Jackson 5
	6/15	2	2	37. You Make Me Feel Brand New	The Stylistics
	11/16	2	2	38. Do It ('Til You're Satisfied)	B.T. Express
	3/09	2	2	39. Boogie Down	Eddie Kendricks
	7/27	2	2	40. Don't Let The Sun Go Down On Me	Elton John

As Recorded By THE FLEETWOODS On Dolphin Records

COME SOFTLY TO ME

By GARY TROXEL • GRETCHEN CHRISTOPHER • BARBARA ELLIS

PRICE **60¢** IN U.S.A.

CORNERSTONE MUSIC CO.
Sole Selling Agent: **MERIDIAN MUSIC CORP.** • 31 WEST 54th STREET, NEW YORK 19, N.Y.

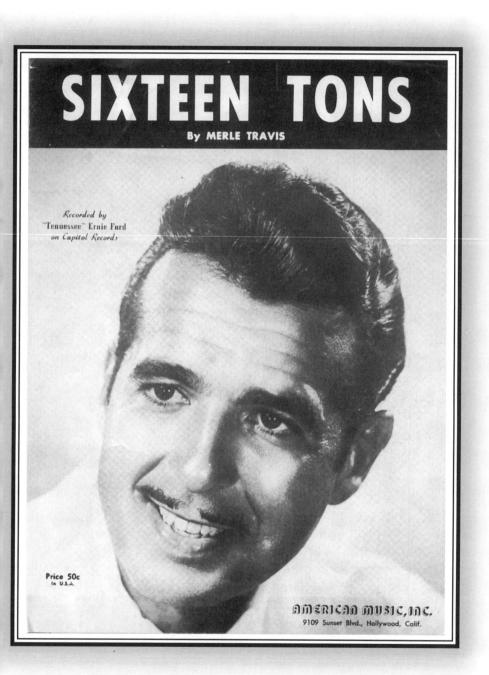

SIXTEEN TONS

By MERLE TRAVIS

Recorded by
"Tennessee" Ernie Ford
on Capitol Records

Price 50c
In U.S.A.

AMERICAN MUSIC, INC.
9109 Sunset Blvd., Hollywood, Calif.

TOP 40 HITS
1975

RANK	PK DATE	PK WKS	PK POS	TITLE	ARTIST
194	6/21	4	1	1. Love Will Keep Us Together	The Captain & Tennille
302	11/29	3	1	2. Fly, Robin, Fly	Silver Convention
306	11/01	3	1	3. Island Girl	Elton John
324	5/03	3	1	4. He Don't Love You (Like I Love You)	Tony Orlando & Dawn
325	10/11	3	1	5. Bad Blood	Neil Sedaka
369	9/06	2	1	6. Rhinestone Cowboy	Glen Campbell
374	4/12	2	1	7. Philadelphia Freedom	The Elton John Band
392	11/22	2	1	8. That's The Way (I Like It)	KC & The Sunshine Band
441	8/09	2	1	9. Jive Talkin'	Bee Gees
510	9/20	2	1	10. Fame	David Bowie
541	1/04	2	1	11. Lucy In The Sky With Diamonds	Elton John
590	8/02	1	1	12. One Of These Nights	Eagles
648	5/31	1	1	13. Before The Next Teardrop Falls	Freddy Fender
654	3/22	1	1	14. My Eyes Adored You	Frankie Valli
668	4/05	1	1	15. Lovin' You	Minnie Riperton
696	2/01	1	1	16. Laughter In The Rain	Neil Sedaka
714	4/26	1	1	17. (Hey Won't You Play) Another Somebody Done Somebody Wrong Song	B.J. Thomas
729	3/29	1	1	18. Lady Marmalade	LaBelle
731	2/22	1	1	19. Pick Up The Pieces	AWB
739	7/26	1	1	20. The Hustle	Van McCoy
740	3/15	1	1	21. Black Water	The Doobie Brothers
744	12/27	1	1	22. Let's Do It Again	The Staple Singers
755	3/08	1	1	23. Have You Never Been Mellow	Olivia Newton-John
758	7/19	1	1	24. Listen To What The Man Said	Wings
795	3/01	1	1	25. Best Of My Love	The Eagles
823	8/23	1	1	26. Fallin' In Love	Hamilton, Joe Frank & Reynold
845	6/07	1	1	27. Thank God I'm A Country Boy	John Denver
846	5/24	1	1	28. Shining Star	Earth, Wind & Fire
857	1/25	1	1	29. Please Mr. Postman	Carpenters
858	1/18	1	1	30. Mandy	Barry Manilow
862	2/15	1	1	31. You're No Good	Linda Ronstadt
871	9/27	1	1	32. I'm Sorry	John Denver
872	2/08	1	1	33. Fire	Ohio Players
873	6/14	1	1	34. Sister Golden Hair	America
874	8/30	1	1	35. Get Down Tonight	K.C. & The Sunshine Band
921	10/11	4	2	36. Calypso	John Denver
997	7/26	3	2	37. I'm Not In Love	10cc
	6/21	2	2	38. When Will I Be Loved	Linda Ronstadt
	1/04	2	2	39. You're The First, The Last, My Everything	Barry White
	11/08	2	2	40. Lyin' Eyes	The Eagles

TOP 40 HITS
1976

RANK	PK DATE	PK WKS	PK POS	TITLE	ARTIST
31	11/13	8	1	1. Tonight's The Night (Gonna Be Alright)	Rod Stewart
95	5/22	5	1	2. Silly Love Songs	Wings
182	8/07	4	1	3. Don't Go Breaking My Heart	Elton John & Kiki Dee
185	4/03	4	1	4. Disco Lady	Johnnie Taylor
227	9/18	3	1	5. Play That Funky Music	Wild Cherry
319	3/13	3	1	6. December, 1963 (Oh, What a Night)	The Four Seasons
320	2/07	3	1	7. 50 Ways To Leave Your Lover	Paul Simon
370	7/24	2	1	8. Kiss And Say Goodbye	Manhattans
375	10/23	2	1	9. If You Leave Me Now	Chicago
388	5/29	2	1	10. Love Hangover	Diana Ross
431	7/10	2	1	11. Afternoon Delight	Starland Vocal Band
575	9/11	1	1	12. (Shake, Shake, Shake) Shake Your Booty	KC & The Sunshine Band
579	10/09	1	1	13. A Fifth Of Beethoven	Walter Murphy/Big Apple Band
583	10/16	1	1	14. Disco Duck (Part 1)	Rick Dees & His Cast Of Idiots
585	1/17	1	1	15. I Write The Songs	Barry Manilow
592	1/31	1	1	16. Love Rollercoaster	Ohio Players
693	5/15	1	1	17. Boogie Fever	Sylvers
732	1/24	1	1	18. Theme From Mahogany (Do You Know Where You're Going To)	Diana Ross
736	9/04	1	1	19. You Should Be Dancing	Bee Gees
738	5/01	1	1	20. Let Your Love Flow	Bellamy Brothers
756	1/10	1	1	21. Convoy	C.W. McCall
759	5/08	1	1	22. Welcome Back	John Sebastian
770	3/06	1	1	23. Love Machine (Part 1)	The Miracles
816	2/28	1	1	24. Theme From S.W.A.T.	Rhythm Heritage
821	1/03	1	1	25. Saturday Night	Bay City Rollers
847	11/06	1	1	26. Rock'n Me	Steve Miller
950	12/04	3	2	27. The Rubberband Man	Spinners
951	6/12	3	2	28. Get Up And Boogie (That's Right)	Silver Convention
958	3/27	3	2	29. Dream Weaver	Gary Wright
980	3/06	3	2	30. All By Myself	Eric Carmen
	9/25	2	2	31. I'd Really Love To See You Tonight	England Dan & John Ford Coley
	5/01	2	2	32. Right Back Where We Started From	Maxine Nightingale
	9/04	2	2	33. You'll Never Find Another Love Like Mine	Lou Rawls
	7/31	2	2	34. Love Is Alive	Gary Wright
	2/07	2	2	35. Love To Love You Baby	Donna Summer
	11/20	2	2	36. The Wreck Of The Edmund Fitzgerald	Gordon Lightfoot
	11/20	4	3	37. Love So Right	Bee Gees
	6/12	4	3	38. Misty Blue	Dorothy Moore
	8/14	4	3	39. Let 'Em In	Wings
	2/07	3	3	40. You Sexy Thing	Hot Chocolate

TOP 40 HITS
1977

RANK	PK DATE	PK WKS	PK POS	TITLE	ARTIST
13	10/15	10	1	1. You Light Up My Life	Debby Boone
89	8/20	5	1	2. Best Of My Love	Emotions
124	7/30	4	1	3. I Just Want To Be Your Everything	Andy Gibb
200	12/24	3	1	4. How Deep Is Your Love	Bee Gees
208	3/05	3	1	5. Love Theme From "A Star Is Born" (Evergreen)	Barbra Streisand
271	5/21	3	1	6. Sir Duke	Stevie Wonder
356	2/05	2	1	7. Torn Between Two Lovers	Mary MacGregor
514	3/26	2	1	8. Rich Girl	Daryl Hall & John Oates
522	10/01	2	1	9. Star Wars Theme/Cantina Band	Meco
616	6/25	1	1	10. Got To Give It Up (Pt. I)	Marvin Gaye
620	1/29	1	1	11. Car Wash	Rose Royce
633	1/08	1	1	12. You Don't Have To Be A Star (To Be In My Show)	Marilyn McCoo & Billy Davis,
637	4/23	1	1	13. Don't Leave Me This Way	Thelma Houston
638	1/15	1	1	14. You Make Me Feel Like Dancing	Leo Sayer
644	4/09	1	1	15. Dancing Queen	Abba
649	4/30	1	1	16. Southern Nights	Glen Campbell
650	2/19	1	1	17. Blinded By The Light	Manfred Mann's Earth Band
651	5/07	1	1	18. Hotel California	Eagles
653	1/22	1	1	19. I Wish	Stevie Wonder
666	7/02	1	1	20. Gonna Fly Now	Bill Conti
681	7/09	1	1	21. Undercover Angel	Alan O'Day
707	5/14	1	1	22. When I Need You	Leo Sayer
724	4/16	1	1	23. Don't Give Up On Us	David Soul
726	6/18	1	1	24. Dreams	Fleetwood Mac
734	2/26	1	1	25. New Kid In Town	Eagles
735	7/16	1	1	26. Da Doo Ron Ron	Shaun Cassidy
772	6/11	1	1	27. I'm Your Boogie Man	KC & The Sunshine Band
851	7/23	1	1	28. Looks Like We Made It	Barry Manilow
941	11/26	3	2	29. Don't It Make My Brown Eyes Blue	Crystal Gayle
957	10/22	3	2	30. Nobody Does It Better	Carly Simon
968	10/01	3	2	31. Keep It Comin' Love	KC & The Sunshine Band
982	7/30	3	2	32. I'm In You	Peter Frampton
	11/12	2	2	33. Boogie Nights	Heatwave
	3/12	2	2	34. Fly Like An Eagle	Steve Miller
	9/17	2	2	35. Float On	The Floaters
	9/10	1	2	36. (Your Love Has Lifted Me) Higher And Higher	Rita Coolidge
	12/17	4	3	37. Blue Bayou	Linda Ronstadt
	1/29	2	3	38. Dazz	Brick
	10/22	2	3	39. That's Rock 'N' Roll	Shaun Cassidy
	9/24	2	3	40. Don't Stop	Fleetwood Mac

TOP 40 HITS
1978

RANK	PK DATE	PK WKS	PK POS	TITLE	ARTIST
29	3/18	8	1	1. Night Fever	Bee Gees
40	6/17	7	1	2. Shadow Dancing	Andy Gibb
58	12/09	6	1	3. Le Freak	Chic
128	2/04	4	1	4. Stayin' Alive	Bee Gees
138	9/30	4	1	5. Kiss You All Over	Exile
214	9/09	3	1	6. Boogie Oogie Oogie	A Taste Of Honey
228	1/14	3	1	7. Baby Come Back	Player
244	11/11	3	1	8. MacArthur Park	Donna Summer
341	3/04	2	1	9. (Love Is) Thicker Than Water	Andy Gibb
344	8/12	2	1	10. Three Times A Lady	Commodores
360	12/02	2	1	11. You Don't Bring Me Flowers	Barbra & Neil
419	8/26	2	1	12. Grease	Frankie Valli
439	5/20	2	1	13. With A Little Luck	Wings
584	5/13	1	1	14. If I Can't Have You	Yvonne Elliman
597	10/28	1	1	15. Hot Child In The City	Nick Gilder
604	6/10	1	1	16. You're The One That I Want	John Travolta & Olivia Newton-John
610	8/05	1	1	17. Miss You	The Rolling Stones
635	11/04	1	1	18. You Needed Me	Anne Murray
676	6/03	1	1	19. Too Much, Too Little, Too Late	Johnny Mathis/ Deniece Williams
888	6/24	6	2	20. Baker Street	Gerry Rafferty
995	1/28	3	2	21. Short People	Randy Newman
	5/13	2	2	22. The Closer I Get To You	Roberta Flack/Donny Hathaway
	11/18	2	2	23. Double Vision	Foreigner
	4/01	3	3	24. Lay Down Sally	Eric Clapton
	4/22	3	3	25. Can't Smile Without You	Barry Manilow
	11/18	3	3	26. How Much I Feel	Ambrosia
	3/18	2	3	27. Emotion	Samantha Sang
	2/18	2	3	28. Just The Way You Are	Billy Joel
	3/04	2	3	29. Sometimes When We Touch	Dan Hill
	9/23	2	3	30. Hopelessly Devoted To You	Olivia Newton-John
	7/08	2	3	31. Take A Chance On Me	Abba
	9/09	2	3	32. Hot Blooded	Foreigner
	8/12	2	3	33. Last Dance	Donna Summer
	10/28	2	3	34. Reminiscing	Little River Band
	6/24	2	3	35. It's A Heartache	Bonnie Tyler
	1/14	2	3	36. Here You Come Again	Dolly Parton
	2/04	3	4	37. We Are The Champions	Queen
	1/14	3	4	38. You're In My Heart (The Final Acclaim)	Rod Stewart
	12/09	2	4	39. I Just Wanna Stop	Gino Vannelli
	7/08	2	4	40. Use Ta Be My Girl	The O'Jays

TOP 40 HITS
1979

RANK	PK DATE	PK WKS	PK POS	TITLE	ARTIST
70	8/25	6	1	1. My Sharona	The Knack
100	7/14	5	1	2. Bad Girls	Donna Summer
137	2/10	4	1	3. Da Ya Think I'm Sexy?	Rod Stewart
151	5/05	4	1	4. Reunited	Peaches & Herb
207	6/02	3	1	5. Hot Stuff	Donna Summer
209	3/10	3	1	6. I Will Survive	Gloria Gaynor
230	12/22	3	1	7. Escape (The Pina Colada Song)	Rupert Holmes
345	6/30	2	1	8. Ring My Bell	Anita Ward
350	12/08	2	1	9. Babe	Styx
376	1/06	2	1	10. Too Much Heaven	Bee Gees
380	10/20	2	1	11. Rise	Herb Alpert
387	3/24	2	1	12. Tragedy	Bee Gees
399	11/24	2	1	13. No More Tears (Enough Is Enough)	Barbra Streisand/ Donna Summer
567	11/17	1	1	14. Still	Commodores
595	11/03	1	1	15. Pop Muzik	M
596	10/06	1	1	16. Sad Eyes	Robert John
622	4/14	1	1	17. What A Fool Believes	The Doobie Brothers
623	8/18	1	1	18. Good Times	Chic
627	11/10	1	1	19. Heartache Tonight	Eagles
703	4/28	1	1	20. Heart Of Glass	Blondie
790	4/21	1	1	21. Knock On Wood	Amii Stewart
818	10/13	1	1	22. Don't Stop 'Til You Get Enough	Michael Jackson
852	6/09	1	1	23. Love You Inside Out	Bee Gees
930	2/03	3	2	24. Y.M.C.A.	Village People
	11/10	2	2	25. Dim All The Lights	Donna Summer
	9/15	2	2	26. After The Love Has Gone	Earth, Wind & Fire
	2/24	2	2	27. Fire	Pointer Sisters
	6/16	2	2	28. We Are Family	Sister Sledge
	8/11	4	3	29. The Main Event/Fight	Barbra Streisand
	1/06	3	3	30. My Life	Billy Joel
	2/17	2	3	31. A Little More Love	Olivia Newton-John
	9/15	2	3	32. The Devil Went Down To Georgia	The Charlie Daniels Band
	5/19	2	3	33. In The Navy	Village People
	5/05	1	3	34. Music Box Dancer	Frank Mills
	12/22	4	4	35. Send One Your Love	Stevie Wonder
	3/17	3	4	36. Heaven Knows	Donna Summer with Brooklyn Dreams
	5/12	2	4	37. Stumblin' In	Suzi Quatro & Chris Norman
	10/13	2	4	38. Sail On	Commodores
	4/07	2	4	39. Sultans Of Swing	Dire Straits
	6/16	2	4	40. Just When I Needed You Most	Randy Vanwarmer

TOP 40 HITS
1980

RANK	PK DATE	PK WKS	PK POS	TITLE	ARTIST
63	11/15	6	1	1. Lady	Kenny Rogers
68	4/19	6	1	2. Call Me	Blondie
85	12/27	5	1	3. (Just Like) Starting Over	John Lennon
126	9/06	4	1	4. Upside Down	Diana Ross
134	3/22	4	1	5. Another Brick In The Wall (Part II)	Pink Floyd
139	2/23	4	1	6. Crazy Little Thing Called Love	Queen
162	1/19	4	1	7. Rock With You	Michael Jackson
163	8/02	4	1	8. Magic	Olivia Newton-John
165	5/31	4	1	9. Funkytown	Lipps, Inc.
204	10/04	3	1	10. Another One Bites The Dust	Queen
216	10/25	3	1	11. Woman In Love	Barbra Streisand
220	6/28	3	1	12. Coming Up (Live at Glasgow)	Paul McCartney & Wings
343	7/19	2	1	13. It's Still Rock And Roll To Me	Billy Joel
560	2/16	1	1	14. Do That To Me One More Time	The Captain & Tennille
573	1/05	1	1	15. Please Don't Go	K.C. & The Sunshine Band
721	8/30	1	1	16. Sailing	Christopher Cross
892	12/06	5	2	17. More Than I Can Say	Leo Sayer
904	9/13	4	2	18. All Out Of Love	Air Supply
908	4/26	4	2	19. Ride Like The Wind	Christopher Cross
	3/29	2	2	20. Working My Way Back To You/ Forgive Me, Girl	Spinners
	3/01	2	2	21. Yes, I'm Ready	Teri DeSario with K.C.
	3/15	2	2	22. Longer	Dan Fogelberg
	7/19	4	3	23. Little Jeannie	Elton John
	1/26	4	3	24. Coward Of The County	Kenny Rogers
	5/03	4	3	25. Lost In Love	Air Supply
	6/28	3	3	26. The Rose	Bette Midler
	6/07	3	3	27. Biggest Part Of Me	Ambrosia
	11/15	3	3	28. The Wanderer	Donna Summer
	10/25	3	3	29. He's So Shy	Pointer Sisters
	9/06	2	3	30. Emotional Rescue	The Rolling Stones
	8/16	2	3	31. Take Your Time (Do It Right) Part 1	The S.O.S. Band
	3/08	4	4	32. Desire	Andy Gibb
	2/02	4	4	33. Cruisin'	Smokey Robinson
	4/19	4	4	34. With You I'm Born Again	Billy Preston & Syreeta
	7/19	3	4	35. Cupid/I've Loved You For A Long Time	Spinners
	5/24	3	4	36. Don't Fall In Love With A Dreamer	Kenny Rogers with Kim Carnes
	9/27	2	4	37. Give Me The Night	George Benson
	9/13	2	4	38. Fame	Irene Cara
	12/27	5	5	39. Hungry Heart	Bruce Springsteen
	12/06	3	5	40. Master Blaster (Jammin')	Stevie Wonder

TOP 40 HITS
1981

RANK	PK DATE	PK WKS	PK POS	TITLE	ARTIST
12	11/21	10	1	1. Physical	Olivia Newton-John
16	5/16	9	1	2. Bette Davis Eyes	Kim Carnes
18	8/15	9	1	3. Endless Love	Diana Ross & Lionel Richie
213	10/17	3	1	4. Arthur's Theme (Best That You Can Do)	Christopher Cross
256	4/11	3	1	5. Kiss On My List	Daryl Hall & John Oates
338	8/01	2	1	6. Jessie's Girl	Rick Springfield
367	2/28	2	1	7. I Love A Rainy Night	Eddie Rabbitt
368	2/21	2	1	8. 9 To 5	Dolly Parton
373	11/07	2	1	9. Private Eyes	Daryl Hall & John Oates
430	3/28	2	1	10. Rapture	Blondie
453	2/07	2	1	11. Celebration	Kool & The Gang
504	5/02	2	1	12. Morning Train (Nine To Five)	Sheena Easton
582	1/31	1	1	13. The Tide Is High	Blondie
594	3/21	1	1	14. Keep On Loving You	REO Speedwagon
657	6/20	1	1	15. Medley	Stars on 45
664	7/25	1	1	16. The One That You Love	Air Supply
877	11/28	10	2	17. Waiting For A Girl Like You	Foreigner
933	3/21	3	2	18. Woman	John Lennon
935	10/31	3	2	19. Start Me Up	The Rolling Stones
937	8/29	3	2	20. Slow Hand	Pointer Sisters
938	5/02	3	2	21. Just The Two Of Us	Grover Washington, Jr. (with Bill Withers)
943	1/10	3	2	22. Love On The Rocks	Neil Diamond
944	5/23	3	2	23. Being With You	Smokey Robinson
987	7/04	3	2	24. All Those Years Ago	George Harrison
	9/19	2	2	25. Queen Of Hearts	Juice Newton
	8/15	2	2	26. Theme From "Greatest American Hero" (Believe It or Not)	Joey Scarbury
	9/05	6	3	27. Stop Draggin' My Heart Around	Stevie Nicks (with Tom Petty & The Heartbreakers)
	12/19	5	3	28. Let's Groove	Earth, Wind & Fire
	3/21	4	3	29. The Best Of Times	Styx
	6/13	3	3	30. Sukiyaki	A Taste Of Honey
	8/15	2	3	31. I Don't Need You	Kenny Rogers
	1/10	2	3	32. Guilty	Barbra Streisand & Barry Gib
	12/05	2	3	33. Every Little Thing She Does Is Magic	The Police
	9/05	4	4	34. Urgent	Foreigner
	5/02	4	4	35. Angel Of The Morning	Juice Newton
	10/17	4	4	36. For Your Eyes Only	Sheena Easton
	12/05	3	4	37. Oh No	Commodores
	10/03	2	4	38. Who's Crying Now	Journey
	6/20	2	4	39. A Woman Needs Love (Just Like You Do)	Ray Parker Jr. & Raydio
	9/05	5	5	40. (There's) No Gettin' Over Me	Ronnie Milsap

TOP 40 HITS
1982

RANK	PK DATE	PK WKS	PK POS	TITLE	ARTIST
43	3/20	7	1	1. I Love Rock 'N Roll	Joan Jett & The Blackhearts
44	5/15	7	1	2. Ebony And Ivory	Paul McCartney/Stevie Wonder
60	7/24	6	1	3. Eye Of The Tiger	Survivor
67	2/06	6	1	4. Centerfold	The J. Geils Band
131	12/18	4	1	5. Maneater	Daryl Hall & John Oates
149	10/02	4	1	6. Jack & Diane	John Cougar
211	7/03	3	1	7. Don't You Want Me	The Human League
292	11/06	3	1	8. Up Where We Belong	Joe Cocker & Jennifer Warnes
335	9/04	2	1	9. Abracadabra	The Steve Miller Band
340	9/11	2	1	10. Hard To Say I'm Sorry	Chicago
364	11/27	2	1	11. Truly	Lionel Richie
570	1/30	1	1	12. I Can't Go For That (No Can Do)	Daryl Hall & John Oates
580	12/11	1	1	13. Mickey	Toni Basil
599	10/30	1	1	14. Who Can It Be Now?	Men At Work
614	5/08	1	1	15. Chariots Of Fire - Titles	Vangelis
887	2/27	6	2	16. Open Arms	Journey
890	7/03	5	2	17. Rosanna	Toto
895	8/07	4	2	18. Hurts So Good	John Cougar
902	5/22	4	2	19. Don't Talk To Strangers	Rick Springfield
940	11/27	3	2	20. Gloria	Laura Branigan
952	4/10	3	2	21. We Got The Beat	Go-Go's
	11/06	4	3	22. Heart Attack	Olivia Newton-John
	10/16	3	3	23. Eye In The Sky	The Alan Parsons Project
	5/22	3	3	24. I've Never Been To Me	Charlene
	2/13	2	3	25. Harden My Heart	Quarterflash
	7/24	7	4	26. Hold Me	Fleetwood Mac
	4/10	4	4	27. Freeze-Frame	The J. Geils Band
	3/20	3	4	28. That Girl	Stevie Wonder
	5/22	3	4	29. 867-5309/Jenny	Tommy Tutone
	2/27	3	4	30. Shake It Up	The Cars
	10/23	3	4	31. I Keep Forgettin' (Every Time You're Near)	Michael McDonald
	6/26	3	4	32. Heat Of The Moment	Asia
	6/12	2	4	33. The Other Woman	Ray Parker Jr.
	11/13	4	5	34. Heartlight	Neil Diamond
	6/12	3	5	35. Always On My Mind	Willie Nelson
	9/18	3	5	36. You Should Hear How She Talks About You	Melissa Manchester
	4/03	3	5	37. Make A Move On Me	Olivia Newton-John
	9/04	2	5	38. Even The Nights Are Better	Air Supply
	3/20	2	5	39. Sweet Dreams	Air Supply
	7/17	2	5	40. Let It Whip	Dazz Band

TOP 40 HITS
1983

RANK	PK DATE	PK WKS	PK POS	TITLE	ARTIST
27	7/09	8	1	1. Every Breath You Take	The Police
47	3/05	7	1	2. Billie Jean	Michael Jackson
61	5/28	6	1	3. Flashdance...What A Feeling	Irene Cara
64	12/10	6	1	4. Say Say Say	Paul McCartney/ Michael Jackson
130	11/12	4	1	5. All Night Long (All Night)	Lionel Richie
141	10/01	4	1	6. Total Eclipse Of The Heart	Bonnie Tyler
147	1/15	4	1	7. Down Under	Men At Work
226	4/30	3	1	8. Beat It	Michael Jackson
339	10/29	2	1	9. Islands In The Stream	Kenny Rogers with Dolly Parton
366	2/19	2	1	10. Baby, Come To Me	Patti Austin with James Ingram
378	9/10	2	1	11. Maniac	Michael Sembello
589	5/21	1	1	12. Let's Dance	David Bowie
600	9/03	1	1	13. Sweet Dreams (Are Made of This)	Eurythmics
697	9/24	1	1	14. Tell Her About It	Billy Joel
773	2/05	1	1	15. Africa	Toto
783	4/23	1	1	16. Come On Eileen	Dexys Midnight Runners
893	7/02	5	2	17. Electric Avenue	Eddy Grant
907	12/17	4	2	18. Say It Isn't So	Daryl Hall & John Oates
913	2/26	4	2	19. Shame On The Moon	Bob Seger & Silver Bullet Band
946	1/08	3	2	20. The Girl Is Mine	Michael Jackson/ Paul McCartney
948	3/26	3	2	21. Do You Really Want To Hurt Me	Culture Club
949	10/08	3	2	22. Making Love Out Of Nothing At All	Air Supply
	6/18	2	2	23. Time (Clock Of The Heart)	Culture Club
	5/07	1	2	24. Jeopardy	Greg Kihn Band
	11/12	5	3	25. Uptown Girl	Billy Joel
	9/10	4	3	26. The Safety Dance	Men Without Hats
	1/29	3	3	27. Sexual Healing	Marvin Gaye
	1/08	3	3	28. Dirty Laundry	Don Henley
	3/26	3	3	29. Hungry Like The Wolf	Duran Duran
	8/06	3	3	30. She Works Hard For The Money	Donna Summer
	12/24	3	3	31. Union Of The Snake	Duran Duran
	2/26	3	3	32. Stray Cat Strut	Stray Cats
	4/16	2	3	33. Mr. Roboto	Styx
	10/08	2	3	34. King Of Pain	The Police
	6/04	1	3	35. Overkill	Men At Work
	7/09	4	4	36. Never Gonna Let You Go	Sergio Mendes
	10/08	4	4	37. True	Spandau Ballet
	9/03	2	4	38. Puttin' On The Ritz	Taco
	3/26	2	4	39. You Are	Lionel Richie
	11/05	1	4	40. One Thing Leads To Another	The Fixx

TOP 40 HITS
1984

RANK	PK DATE	PK WKS	PK POS	TITLE	ARTIST
78	12/22	6	1	1. Like A Virgin	Madonna
91	7/07	5	1	2. When Doves Cry	Prince
99	2/25	5	1	3. Jump	Van Halen
219	3/31	3	1	4. Footloose	Kenny Loggins
225	9/01	3	1	5. What's Love Got To Do With It	Tina Turner
229	4/21	3	1	6. Against All Odds (Take A Look At Me Now)	Phil Collins
232	10/13	3	1	7. I Just Called To Say I Love You	Stevie Wonder
235	8/11	3	1	8. Ghostbusters	Ray Parker Jr.
243	2/04	3	1	9. Karma Chameleon	Culture Club
260	11/17	3	1	10. Wake Me Up Before You Go-Go	Wham!
353	5/12	2	1	11. Hello	Lionel Richie
354	1/21	2	1	12. Owner Of A Lonely Heart	Yes
377	12/08	2	1	13. Out Of Touch	Daryl Hall/John Oates
382	6/09	2	1	14. Time After Time	Cyndi Lauper
383	5/26	2	1	15. Let's Hear It For The Boy	Deniece Williams
384	9/29	2	1	16. Let's Go Crazy	Prince & the Revolution
421	6/23	2	1	17. The Reflex	Duran Duran
456	11/03	2	1	18. Caribbean Queen (No More Love On The Run)	Billy Ocean
605	9/22	1	1	19. Missing You	John Waite
909	6/30	4	2	20. Dancing In The Dark	Bruce Springsteen
914	12/15	4	2	21. The Wild Boys	Duran Duran
960	3/24	3	2	22. Somebody's Watching Me	Rockwell
	3/10	2	2	23. Girls Just Want To Have Fun	Cyndi Lauper
	11/17	2	2	24. Purple Rain	Prince & the Revolution
	2/11	1	2	25. Joanna	Kool & The Gang
	3/03	1	2	26. 99 Luftballons	Nena
	11/24	3	3	27. I Feel For You	Chaka Khan
	9/08	3	3	28. She Bop	Cyndi Lauper
	1/28	3	3	29. Talking In Your Sleep	The Romantics
	9/29	3	3	30. Drive	The Cars
	8/04	3	3	31. State Of Shock	Jacksons
	7/07	2	3	32. Jump (For My Love)	Pointer Sisters
	5/05	2	3	33. Hold Me Now	Thompson Twins
	8/25	2	3	34. Stuck On You	Lionel Richie
	10/20	2	3	35. Hard Habit To Break	Chicago
	6/09	1	3	36. Oh Sherrie	Steve Perry
	3/31	2	4	37. Here Comes The Rain Again	Eurythmics
	6/30	2	4	38. Self Control	Laura Branigan
	7/14	2	4	39. Eyes Without A Face	Billy Idol
	3/03	2	4	40. Thriller	Michael Jackson

TOP 40 HITS
1985

RANK	PK DATE	PK WKS	PK POS	TITLE	ARTIST
164	12/21	4	1	1. Say You, Say Me	Lionel Richie
187	4/13	4	1	2. We Are The World	USA for Africa
242	2/16	3	1	3. Careless Whisper	Wham!/George Michael
262	3/09	3	1	4. Can't Fight This Feeling	REO Speedwagon
269	9/21	3	1	5. Money For Nothing	Dire Straits
300	8/03	3	1	6. Shout	Tears For Fears
381	12/07	2	1	7. Broken Wings	Mr. Mister
415	2/02	2	1	8. I Want To Know What Love Is	Foreigner
422	8/24	2	1	9. The Power Of Love	Huey Lewis & The News
426	6/08	2	1	10. Everybody Wants To Rule The World	Tears For Fears
457	11/16	2	1	11. We Built This City	Starship
466	9/07	2	1	12. St. Elmo's Fire (Man In Motion)	John Parr
513	5/25	2	1	13. Everything She Wants	Wham!
515	6/22	2	1	14. Heaven	Bryan Adams
526	7/13	2	1	15. A View To A Kill	Duran Duran
531	3/30	2	1	16. One More Night	Phil Collins
608	11/30	1	1	17. Separate Lives	Phil Collins & Marilyn Martin
621	5/11	1	1	18. Crazy For You	Madonna
643	7/27	1	1	19. Everytime You Go Away	Paul Young
655	5/18	1	1	20. Don't You (Forget About Me)	Simple Minds
658	11/02	1	1	21. Part-Time Lover	Stevie Wonder
686	10/19	1	1	22. Take On Me	a-ha
691	10/26	1	1	23. Saving All My Love For You	Whitney Houston
719	11/09	1	1	24. Miami Vice Theme	Jan Hammer
798	7/06	1	1	25. Sussudio	Phil Collins
801	10/12	1	1	26. Oh Sheila	Ready For The World
953	12/28	3	2	27. Party All The Time	Eddie Murphy
967	9/21	3	2	28. Cherish	Kool & The Gang
	2/02	2	2	29. Easy Lover	Philip Bailey/Phil Collins
	11/16	2	2	30. You Belong To The City	Glenn Frey
	1/12	2	2	31. All I Need	Jack Wagner
	3/23	2	2	32. Material Girl	Madonna
	2/23	1	2	33. Loverboy	Billy Ocean
	7/20	1	2	34. Raspberry Beret	Prince & the Revolution
	3/16	1	2	35. The Heat Is On	Glenn Frey
	9/14	1	2	36. We Don't Need Another Hero (Thunderdome)	Tina Turner
	6/01	3	3	37. Axel F	Harold Faltermeyer
	4/27	2	3	38. Rhythm Of The Night	DeBarge
	12/28	2	3	39. Alive & Kicking	Simple Minds
	1/19	2	3	40. You're The Inspiration	Chicago

TOP 40 HITS
1986

RANK	PK DATE	PK WKS	PK POS	TITLE	ARTIST
148	1/18	4	1	1. That's What Friends Are For	Dionne & Friends
181	12/20	4	1	2. Walk Like An Egyptian	Bangles
293	6/14	3	1	3. On My Own	Patti LaBelle/ Michael McDonald
297	5/17	3	1	4. Greatest Love Of All	Whitney Houston
301	9/20	3	1	5. Stuck With You	Huey Lewis & the News
303	3/29	3	1	6. Rock Me Amadeus	Falco
472	3/01	2	1	7. Kyrie	Mr. Mister
473	4/19	2	1	8. Kiss	Prince & The Revolution
474	8/16	2	1	9. Papa Don't Preach	Madonna
501	2/15	2	1	10. How Will I Know	Whitney Houston
509	8/02	2	1	11. Glory Of Love	Peter Cetera
523	10/11	2	1	12. When I Think Of You	Janet Jackson
530	10/25	2	1	13. True Colors	Cyndi Lauper
532	11/08	2	1	14. Amanda	Boston
645	12/13	1	1	15. The Way It Is	Bruce Hornsby & The Range
695	11/22	1	1	16. Human	Human League
701	5/03	1	1	17. Addicted To Love	Robert Palmer
704	7/05	1	1	18. There'll Be Sad Songs (To Make You Cry)	Billy Ocean
705	7/26	1	1	19. Sledgehammer	Peter Gabriel
706	5/10	1	1	20. West End Girls	Pet Shop Boys
720	9/13	1	1	21. Take My Breath Away	Berlin
723	3/15	1	1	22. Sara	Starship
737	9/06	1	1	23. Venus	Bananarama
780	12/06	1	1	24. The Next Time I Fall	Peter Cetera w/Amy Grant
782	11/29	1	1	25. You Give Love A Bad Name	Bon Jovi
784	7/12	1	1	26. Holding Back The Years	Simply Red
785	8/30	1	1	27. Higher Love	Steve Winwood
803	3/22	1	1	28. These Dreams	Heart
806	6/07	1	1	29. Live To Tell	Madonna
822	7/19	1	1	30. Invisible Touch	Genesis
984	10/18	3	2	31. Typical Male	Tina Turner
	9/13	2	2	32. Dancing On The Ceiling	Lionel Richie
	12/27	2	2	33. Everybody Have Fun Tonight	Wang Chung
	9/27	2	2	34. Friends And Lovers	Gloria Loring & Carl Anderson
	2/01	2	2	35. Burning Heart	Survivor
	7/26	1	2	36. Danger Zone	Kenny Loggins
	10/11	1	2	37. Don't Forget Me (When I'm Gone)	Glass Tiger
	2/15	1	2	38. When The Going Gets Tough, The Tough Get Going	Billy Ocean
	4/19	1	2	39. Manic Monday	Bangles
	11/08	1	2	40. I Didn't Mean To Turn You On	Robert Palmer

TOP 40 HITS
1987

RANK	PK DATE	PK WKS	PK POS	TITLE	ARTIST
166	12/12	4	1	1. Faith	George Michael
193	2/14	4	1	2. Livin' On A Prayer	Bon Jovi
259	7/11	3	1	3. Alone	Heart
270	5/16	3	1	4. With Or Without You	U2
295	8/29	3	1	5. La Bamba	Los Lobos
385	6/27	2	1	6. I Wanna Dance With Somebody (Who Loves Me)	Whitney Houston
420	4/04	2	1	7. Nothing's Gonna Stop Us Now	Starship
476	8/08	2	1	8. I Still Haven't Found What I'm Looking For	U2
478	9/26	2	1	9. Didn't We Almost Have It All	Whitney Houston
481	4/18	2	1	10. I Knew You Were Waiting (For Me)	Aretha Franklin & George Michael
502	1/24	2	1	11. At This Moment	Billy Vera & The Beaters
520	11/07	2	1	12. I Think We're Alone Now	Tiffany
524	5/02	2	1	13. (I Just) Died In Your Arms	Cutting Crew
534	3/21	2	1	14. Lean On Me	Club Nouveau
550	10/24	2	1	15. Bad	Michael Jackson
639	1/17	1	1	16. Shake You Down	Gregory Abbott
698	10/10	1	1	17. Here I Go Again	Whitesnake
702	6/13	1	1	18. Always	Atlantic Starr
708	6/20	1	1	19. Head To Toe	Lisa Lisa & Cult Jam
712	8/01	1	1	20. Shakedown	Bob Seger
778	12/05	1	1	21. Heaven Is A Place On Earth	Belinda Carlisle
779	11/28	1	1	22. (I've Had) The Time Of My Life	Bill Medley & Jennifer Warnes
797	2/07	1	1	23. Open Your Heart	Madonna
802	6/06	1	1	24. You Keep Me Hangin' On	Kim Wilde
804	10/17	1	1	25. Lost In Emotion	Lisa Lisa & Cult Jam
817	11/21	1	1	26. Mony Mony "Live"	Billy Idol
829	3/14	1	1	27. Jacob's Ladder	Huey Lewis & the News
833	8/22	1	1	28. Who's That Girl	Madonna
835	9/19	1	1	29. I Just Can't Stop Loving You	Michael Jackson
919	5/02	4	2	30. Looking For A New Love	Jody Watley
996	10/24	3	2	31. Causing A Commotion	Madonna
	1/17	2	2	32. C'est La Vie	Robbie Nevil
	4/25	1	2	33. Don't Dream It's Over	Crowded House
	12/19	1	2	34. Is This Love	Whitesnake
	8/08	1	2	35. I Want Your Sex	George Michael
	10/17	1	2	36. U Got The Look	Prince
	1/10	1	2	37. Notorious	Duran Duran
	2/21	1	2	38. Keep Your Hands To Yourself	Georgia Satellites
	3/14	1	2	39. Somewhere Out There	Linda Ronstadt & James Ingram
	3/21	1	2	40. Let's Wait Awhile	Janet Jackson

TOP 40 HITS
1988

RANK	PK DATE	PK WKS	PK POS	TITLE	ARTIST
192	7/30	4	1	1. Roll With It	Steve Winwood
261	12/24	3	1	2. Every Rose Has Its Thorn	Poison
298	5/28	3	1	3. One More Try	George Michael
413	12/10	2	1	4. Look Away	Chicago
463	3/12	2	1	5. Never Gonna Give You Up	Rick Astley
464	9/10	2	1	6. Sweet Child O' Mine	Guns N' Roses
465	5/14	2	1	7. Anything For You	Gloria Estefan
469	4/09	2	1	8. Get Outta My Dreams, Get Into My Car	Billy Ocean
477	3/26	2	1	9. Man In The Mirror	Michael Jackson
505	7/09	2	1	10. The Flame	Cheap Trick
512	2/06	2	1	11. Could've Been	Tiffany
518	9/24	2	1	12. Don't Worry Be Happy	Bobby McFerrin
519	10/22	2	1	13. Groovy Kind Of Love	Phil Collins
525	4/23	2	1	14. Where Do Broken Hearts Go	Whitney Houston
527	2/27	2	1	15. Father Figure	George Michael
529	11/19	2	1	16. Bad Medicine	Bon Jovi
536	8/27	2	1	17. Monkey	George Michael
636	1/30	1	1	18. Need You Tonight	INXS
646	1/16	1	1	19. Got My Mind Set On You	George Harrison
663	1/09	1	1	20. So Emotional	Whitney Houston
682	11/12	1	1	21. Wild, Wild West	The Escape Club
771	10/15	1	1	22. Red Red Wine	UB40
774	2/20	1	1	23. Seasons Change	Exposé
775	5/07	1	1	24. Wishing Well	Terence Trent D'Arby
776	12/03	1	1	25. Baby, I Love Your Way/Freebird Medley (Free Baby)	Will To Power
788	7/23	1	1	26. Hold On To The Nights	Richard Marx
792	6/25	1	1	27. Foolish Beat	Debbie Gibson
799	10/08	1	1	28. Love Bites	Def Leppard
807	1/23	1	1	29. The Way You Make Me Feel	Michael Jackson
820	6/18	1	1	30. Together Forever	Rick Astley
844	11/05	1	1	31. Kokomo	The Beach Boys
860	7/02	1	1	32. Dirty Diana	Michael Jackson
983	5/14	3	2	33. Shattered Dreams	Johnny Hates Jazz
	8/06	2	2	34. Hands To Heaven	Breathe
	3/26	2	2	35. Endless Summer Nights	Richard Marx
	9/10	2	2	36. Simply Irresistible	Robert Palmer
	2/20	2	2	37. What Have I Done To Deserve This?	Pet Shop Boys/Dusty Springfield
	4/16	2	2	38. Devil Inside	INXS
	7/09	2	2	39. Mercedes Boy	Pebbles
	7/23	1	2	40. Pour Some Sugar On Me	Def Leppard

TOP 40 HITS
1989

RANK	PK DATE	PK WKS	PK POS	TITLE	ARTIST
154	12/23	4	1	1. Another Day In Paradise	Phil Collins
184	10/07	4	1	2. Miss You Much	Janet Jackson
290	2/11	3	1	3. Straight Up	Paula Abdul
299	8/12	3	1	4. Right Here Waiting	Richard Marx
304	3/04	3	1	5. Lost In Your Eyes	Debbie Gibson
305	4/22	3	1	6. Like A Prayer	Madonna
423	12/09	2	1	7. We Didn't Start The Fire	Billy Joel
475	1/21	2	1	8. Two Hearts	Phil Collins
503	11/11	2	1	9. When I See You Smile	Bad English
506	11/25	2	1	10. Blame It On The Rain	Milli Vanilli
507	5/20	2	1	11. Forever Your Girl	Paula Abdul
508	9/23	2	1	12. Girl I'm Gonna Miss You	Milli Vanilli
521	7/22	2	1	13. Toy Soldiers	Martika
647	9/02	1	1	14. Cold Hearted	Paula Abdul
667	9/16	1	1	15. Don't Wanna Lose You	Gloria Estefan
685	6/10	1	1	16. Wind Beneath My Wings	Bette Midler
688	1/14	1	1	17. My Prerogative	Bobby Brown
700	4/15	1	1	18. She Drives Me Crazy	Fine Young Cannibals
725	4/08	1	1	19. The Look	Roxette
777	7/15	1	1	20. If You Don't Know Me By Now	Simply Red
786	11/04	1	1	21. Listen To Your Heart	Roxette
787	6/17	1	1	22. I'll Be Loving You (Forever)	New Kids On The Block
789	7/01	1	1	23. Baby Don't Forget My Number	Milli Vanilli
791	3/25	1	1	24. The Living Years	Mike & The Mechanics
796	4/01	1	1	25. Eternal Flame	Bangles
800	5/13	1	1	26. I'll Be There For You	Bon Jovi
810	7/08	1	1	27. Good Thing	Fine Young Cannibals
824	9/09	1	1	28. Hangin' Tough	New Kids On The Block
831	8/05	1	1	29. Batdance	Prince
849	2/04	1	1	30. When I'm With You	Sheriff
850	6/03	1	1	31. Rock On	Michael Damian
855	6/24	1	1	32. Satisfied	Richard Marx
981	8/05	3	2	33. On Our Own	Bobby Brown
	12/23	2	2	34. Don't Know Much	Linda Ronstadt feat. Aaron Neville
	9/23	2	2	35. Heaven	Warrant
	5/20	2	2	36. Real Love	Jody Watley
	10/07	2	2	37. Cherish	Madonna
	7/15	2	2	38. Express Yourself	Madonna
	4/01	1	2	39. Girl You Know It's True	Milli Vanilli
	1/21	1	2	40. Don't Rush Me	Taylor Dayne

TOP 40 HITS
1990

RANK	PK DATE	PK WKS	PK POS	TITLE	ARTIST
150	12/08	4	1	1. Because I Love You (The Postman Song)	Stevie B
152	4/21	4	1	2. Nothing Compares 2 U	Sinéad O'Connor
191	8/04	4	1	3. Vision Of Love	Mariah Carey
257	5/19	3	1	4. Vogue	Madonna
263	3/03	3	1	5. Escapade	Janet Jackson
289	11/10	3	1	6. Love Takes Time	Mariah Carey
294	2/10	3	1	7. Opposites Attract	Paula Abdul with The Wild Pair
311	6/30	3	1	8. Step By Step	New Kids On The Block
318	1/20	3	1	9. How Am I Supposed To Live Without You	Michael Bolton
372	6/16	2	1	10. It Must Have Been Love	Roxette
458	3/24	2	1	11. Black Velvet	Alannah Myles
460	9/15	2	1	12. Release Me	Wilson Phillips
471	7/21	2	1	13. She Ain't Worth It	Glenn Medeiros/Bobby Brown
598	6/09	1	1	14. Hold On	Wilson Phillips
659	9/08	1	1	15. Blaze Of Glory	Jon Bon Jovi
662	12/01	1	1	16. I'm Your Baby Tonight	Whitney Houston
680	10/06	1	1	17. Close To You	Maxi Priest
687	10/20	1	1	18. I Don't Have The Heart	James Ingram
692	11/03	1	1	19. Ice Ice Baby	Vanilla Ice
699	9/29	1	1	20. (Can't Live Without Your) Love And Affection	Nelson
722	9/01	1	1	21. If Wishes Came True	Sweet Sensation
781	4/07	1	1	22. Love Will Lead You Back	Taylor Dayne
838	10/13	1	1	23. Praying For Time	George Michael
853	4/14	1	1	24. I'll Be Your Everything	Tommy Page
859	10/27	1	1	25. Black Cat	Janet Jackson
979	4/14	3	2	26. Don't Wanna Fall In Love	Jane Child
	1/20	2	2	27. Pump Up The Jam	Technotronic Feat. Felly
	5/26	2	2	28. All I Wanna Do Is Make Love To You	Heart
	2/10	2	2	29. Two To Make It Right	Seduction
	1/06	2	2	30. Rhythm Nation	Janet Jackson
	3/03	2	2	31. Dangerous	Roxette
	8/18	2	2	32. Come Back To Me	Janet Jackson
	11/10	2	2	33. Pray	M.C. Hammer
	12/15	1	2	34. From A Distance	Bette Midler
	8/04	1	2	35. Cradle Of Love	Billy Idol
	7/21	1	2	36. Hold On	En Vogue
	8/11	1	2	37. The Power	Snap!
	5/05	1	2	38. I Wanna Be Rich	Calloway
	11/24	1	2	39. More Than Words Can Say	Alias
	6/09	4	3	40. Poison	Bell Biv DeVoe

TOP 40 HITS
1991

RANK	PK DATE	PK WKS	PK POS	TITLE	ARTIST
49	7/27	7	1	1. (Everything I Do) I Do It For You	Bryan Adams
50	12/07	7	1	2. Black Or White	Michael Jackson
109	6/15	5	1	3. Rush, Rush	Paula Abdul
288	10/12	3	1	4. Emotions	Mariah Carey
371	2/09	2	1	5. Gonna Make You Sweat (Everybody Dance Now)	C & C Music Factory
412	1/26	2	1	6. The First Time	Surface
432	5/25	2	1	7. I Don't Wanna Cry	Mariah Carey
436	1/05	2	1	8. Justify My Love	Madonna
454	4/27	2	1	9. Baby Baby	Amy Grant
455	11/09	2	1	10. Cream	Prince & The N.P.G.
459	2/23	2	1	11. All The Man That I Need	Whitney Houston
462	3/09	2	1	12. Someday	Mariah Carey
467	9/21	2	1	13. I Adore Mi Amor	Color Me Badd
470	3/30	2	1	14. Coming Out Of The Dark	Gloria Estefan
601	6/08	1	1	15. More Than Words	Extreme
602	5/18	1	1	16. I Like The Way (The Kissing Game)	Hi-Five
603	3/23	1	1	17. One More Try	Timmy -T-
606	7/20	1	1	18. Unbelievable	EMF
609	11/23	1	1	19. When A Man Loves A Woman	Michael Bolton
634	11/30	1	1	20. Set Adrift On Memory Bliss	PM Dawn
679	11/02	1	1	21. Romantic	Karyn White
690	1/19	1	1	22. Love Will Never Do (Without You)	Janet Jackson
694	10/05	1	1	23. Good Vibrations	Marky Mark & Funky Bunch
711	4/20	1	1	24. You're In Love	Wilson Phillips
793	5/11	1	1	25. Joyride	Roxette
794	4/13	1	1	26. I've Been Thinking About You	Londonbeat
854	9/14	1	1	27. The Promise Of A New Day	Paula Abdul
900	12/14	4	2	28. It's So Hard To Say Goodbye To Yesterday	Boyz II Men
905	6/08	4	2	29. I Wanna Sex You Up	Color Me Badd
	10/19	2	2	30. Do Anything	Natural Selection feat. Niki Haris
	5/18	2	2	31. Touch Me (All Night Long)	Cathy Dennis
	8/03	2	2	32. P.A.S.S.I.O.N.	Rythm Syndicate
	7/27	1	2	33. Right Here, Right Now	Jesus Jones
	11/16	1	2	34. Can't Stop This Thing We Started	Bryan Adams
	8/17	1	2	35. Every Heartbeat	Amy Grant
	8/24	1	2	36. It Ain't Over 'Til It's Over	Lenny Kravitz
	8/31	1	2	37. Fading Like A Flower (Every Time You Leave)	Roxette
	9/07	3	3	38. Motownphilly	Boyz II Men
	1/12	2	3	39. High Enough	Damn Yankees
	4/13	1	3	40. Hold You Tight	Tara Kemp

TOP 40 HITS
1992

RANK	PK DATE	PK WKS	PK POS	TITLE	ARTIST
4	11/28	14	1	1. I Will Always Love You	Whitney Houston
5	8/15	13	1	2. End of the Road	Boyz II Men
28	4/25	8	1	3. Jump	Kris Kross
82	7/04	5	1	4. Baby Got Back	Sir Mix-A-Lot
87	3/21	5	1	5. Save The Best For Last	Vanessa Williams
215	2/08	3	1	6. I'm Too Sexy	Right Said Fred
240	2/29	3	1	7. To Be With You	Mr. Big
358	11/14	2	1	8. How Do You Talk To An Angel	The Heights
429	6/20	2	1	9. I'll Be There	Mariah Carey
559	1/25	1	1	10. All 4 Love	Color Me Badd
641	2/01	1	1	11. Don't Let The Sun Go Down On Me	George Michael/Elton John
660	8/08	1	1	12. This Used To Be My Playground	Madonna
879	11/21	8	2	13. If I Ever Fall In Love	Shai
885	8/15	6	2	14. Baby-Baby-Baby	TLC
886	9/26	6	2	15. Sometimes Love Just Ain't Enough	Patty Smyth with Don Henley
898	3/28	4	2	16. Tears In Heaven	Eric Clapton
925	12/26	3	2	17. Rump Shaker	Wreckx-N-Effect
929	5/16	3	2	18. My Lovin' (You're Never Gonna Get It)	En Vogue
934	2/01	3	2	19. I Love Your Smile	Shanice
	6/06	1	2	20. Under The Bridge	Red Hot Chili Peppers
	1/25	1	2	21. Can't Let Go	Mariah Carey
	5/09	1	2	22. Bohemian Rhapsody	Queen
	10/31	4	3	23. I'd Die Without You	PM Dawn
	3/07	4	3	24. Remember The Time	Michael Jackson
	9/12	3	3	25. Humpin' Around	Bobby Brown
	10/10	2	3	26. Jump Around	House Of Pain
	8/29	2	3	27. November Rain	Guns N' Roses
	4/11	1	3	28. Masterpiece	Atlantic Starr
	2/15	1	3	29. Diamonds And Pearls	Prince & The N.P.G.
	10/24	1	3	30. Erotica	Madonna
	7/18	3	4	31. Achy Breaky Heart	Billy Ray Cyrus
	5/23	2	4	32. Live And Learn	Joe Public
	7/11	1	4	33. If You Asked Me To	Celine Dion
	9/19	1	4	34. Stay	Shakespear's Sister
	1/18	2	5	35. Finally	Ce Ce Peniston
	6/27	2	5	36. Damn I Wish I Was Your Lover	Sophie B. Hawkins
	8/01	1	5	37. Just Another Day	Jon Secada
	10/17	1	5	38. She's Playing Hard To Get	Hi-Five
	4/11	1	5	39. Make It Happen	Mariah Carey
	1/11	1	5	40. 2 Legit 2 Quit	Hammer

TOP 40 HITS
1993

RANK	PK DATE	PK WKS	PK POS	TITLE	ARTIST
25	9/11	8	1	1. Dreamlover	Mariah Carey
26	5/15	8	1	2. That's The Way Love Goes	Janet Jackson
35	7/24	7	1	3. Can't Help Falling In Love	UB40
39	3/13	7	1	4. Informer	Snow
86	11/06	5	1	5. I'd Do Anything For Love (But I Won't Do That)	Meat Loaf
123	12/25	4	1	6. Hero	Mariah Carey
328	5/01	2	1	7. Freak Me	Silk
331	7/10	2	1	8. Weak	SWV (Sisters With Voices)
332	12/11	2	1	9. Again	Janet Jackson
581	3/06	1	1	10. A Whole New World (Aladdin's Theme)	Peabo Bryson & Regina Belle
881	7/31	7	2	11. Whoomp! (There It Is)	Tag Team
922	11/06	3	2	12. All That She Wants	Ace Of Base
947	10/02	3	2	13. Right Here/Human Nature	SWV-Sisters With Voices
	3/20	1	2	14. Nuthin' But A "G" Thang	Dr. Dre
	10/23	1	2	15. Just Kickin' It	Xscape
	5/22	7	3	16. Knockin' Da Boots	H-Town
	1/16	3	3	17. In The Still Of The Nite (I'll Remember)	Boyz II Men
	2/20	3	3	18. Ordinary World	Duran Duran
	10/16	1	3	19. The River Of Dreams	Billy Joel
	5/15	1	3	20. Love Is	Vanessa Williams & Brian McKnight
	8/21	1	3	21. I'm Gonna Be (500 Miles)	The Proclaimers
	4/03	5	4	22. I Have Nothing	Whitney Houston
	9/11	2	4	23. If	Janet Jackson
	11/20	2	4	24. Gangsta Lean	D.R.S.
	1/30	2	4	25. Saving Forever For You	Shanice
	8/28	2	4	26. Lately	Jodeci
	2/20	2	4	27. I'm Every Woman	Whitney Houston
	3/27	1	4	28. Don't Walk Away	Jade
	12/04	1	4	29. Shoop	Salt-N-Pepa
	8/21	1	4	30. Slam	Onyx
	8/28	3	5	31. Runaway Train	Soul Asylum
	6/19	3	5	32. Have I Told You Lately	Rod Stewart
	1/02	1	5	33. Rhythm Is A Dancer	Snap!
	6/12	1	5	34. Show Me Love	Robin S
	5/22	2	6	35. I'm So Into You	SWV
	2/20	2	6	36. Mr. Wendal	Arrested Development
	5/29	2	6	37. Looking Through Patient Eyes	PM Dawn
	10/30	2	6	38. Hey Mr. D.J.	Zhané
	4/10	1	6	39. Cats In The Cradle	Ugly Kid Joe
	8/07	3	7	40. If I Had No Loot	Tony Toni Tone

TOP 40 HITS
1994

RANK	PK DATE	PK WKS	PK POS	TITLE	ARTIST
3	8/27	14	1	1. I'll Make Love To You	Boyz II Men
8	5/21	11	1	2. I Swear	All-4-One
51	3/12	6	1	3. The Sign	Ace Of Base
53	12/03	6	1	4. On Bended Knee	Boyz II Men
122	2/12	4	1	5. The Power Of Love	Celine Dion
132	4/09	4	1	6. Bump N' Grind	R. Kelly
201	8/06	3	1	7. Stay (I Missed You)	Lisa Loeb & Nine Stories
205	1/22	3	1	8. All For Love	Bryan Adams/ Rod Stewart/Sting
330	12/17	2	1	9. Here Comes The Hotstepper	Ini Kamoze
884	10/08	6	2	10. All I Wanna Do	Sheryl Crow
903	5/28	4	2	11. I'll Remember	Madonna
936	7/02	3	2	12. Regulate	Warren G. & Nate Dogg
	6/25	1	2	13. Any Time, Any Place	Janet Jackson
	10/01	1	2	14. Endless Love	Luther Vandross & Mariah Carey
	11/12	11	3	15. Another Night	Real McCoy
	3/19	6	3	16. Without You	Mariah Carey
	7/30	5	3	17. Fantastic Voyage	Coolio
	1/22	3	3	18. Breathe Again	Toni Braxton
	2/26	3	3	19. Whatta Man	Salt 'N' Pepa with En Vogue
	4/30	3	3	20. The Most Beautiful Girl In The World	♀
	9/03	2	3	21. Wild Night	John Mellencamp/ Me'Shell Ndegéocello
	11/05	1	3	22. Secret	Madonna
	9/17	1	3	23. Stroke You Up	Changing Faces
	12/10	6	4	24. Always	Bon Jovi
	9/10	5	4	25. When Can I See You	Babyface
	6/18	4	4	26. Don't Turn Around	Ace Of Base
	4/16	2	4	27. Mmm Mmm Mmm Mmm	Crash Test Dummies
	5/07	2	4	28. Return To Innocence	Enigma
	8/06	1	4	29. Can You Feel The Love Tonight	Elton John
	3/12	3	5	30. So Much In Love	All-4-One
	7/02	1	5	31. Back & Forth	Aaliyah
	10/15	1	5	32. Never Lie	Immature
	5/14	4	6	33. Baby, I Love Your Way	Big Mountain
	12/31	3	6	34. I Wanna Be Down	Brandy
	1/22	2	6	35. Said I Loved You...But I Lied	Michael Bolton
	10/15	2	6	36. At Your Best (You Are Love)	Aaliyah
	8/13	1	6	37. Funkdafied	Da Brat
	5/28	4	7	38. You Mean The World To Me	Toni Braxton
	3/19	3	7	39. Now and Forever	Richard Marx
	2/12	1	7	40. Getto Jam	Domino

TOP 40 HITS
1995

RANK	PK DATE	PK WKS	PK POS	TITLE	ARTIST
1	12/02	16	1	1. One Sweet Day	Mariah Carey & Boyz II Men
21	9/30	8	1	2. Fantasy	Mariah Carey
32	7/08	7	1	3. Waterfalls	TLC
34	2/25	7	1	4. Take A Bow	Madonna
37	4/15	7	1	5. This Is How We Do It	Montell Jordan
88	6/03	5	1	6. Have You Ever Really Loved A Woman?	Bryan Adams
119	1/28	4	1	7. Creep	TLC
198	9/09	3	1	8. Gangsta's Paradise	Coolio Featuring L.V.
556	8/26	1	1	9. Kiss From A Rose	Seal
557	11/25	1	1	10. Exhale (Shoop Shoop)	Whitney Houston
588	9/02	1	1	11. You Are Not Alone	Michael Jackson
899	3/18	4	2	12. Candy Rain	Soul For Real
927	7/01	3	2	13. Don't Take It Personal (just one of dem days)	Monica
932	4/15	3	2	14. Red Light Special	TLC
942	7/15	3	2	15. One More Chance/Stay With Me	The Notorious B.I.G.
	5/06	2	2	16. Freak Like Me	Adina Howard
	6/17	1	2	17. Water Runs Dry	Boyz II Men
	6/24	1	2	18. Total Eclipse Of The Heart	Nicki French
	12/02	8	3	19. Hey Lover	LL Cool J
	10/21	5	3	20. Runaway	Janet Jackson
	8/19	2	3	21. Boombastic	Shaggy
	4/08	1	3	22. Run Away	Real McCoy
	6/03	1	3	23. I'll Be There For You/ You're All I Need To Get By	Method Man featuring Mary J. Blige
	5/06	2	4	24. I Know	Dionne Farris
	3/11	2	4	25. Baby	Brandy
	11/18	2	4	26. You Remind Me Of Something	R. Kelly
	8/26	1	4	27. Colors Of The Wind	Vanessa Williams
	3/25	3	5	28. Strong Enough	Sheryl Crow
	12/30	3	5	29. Diggin' On You	TLC
	11/04	3	5	30. Tell Me	Groove Theory
	6/17	2	5	31. Scream	Michael Jackson & Janet Jackson
	8/26	1	5	32. I Can Love You Like That	All-4-One
	3/11	1	5	33. You Gotta Be	Des'ree
	10/28	3	6	34. As I Lay Me Down	Sophie B. Hawkins
	3/18	2	6	35. Big Poppa	The Notorious B.I.G.
	10/21	1	6	36. Only Wanna Be With You	Hootie & The Blowfish
	12/16	1	6	37. You'll See	Madonna
	1/07	4	7	38. Before I Let You Go	BLACKstreet
	11/11	2	7	39. Back For Good	Take That
	12/30	1	7	40. Before You Walk Out Of My Life	Monica

TOP 40 HITS
1996

RANK	PK DATE	PK WKS	PK POS	TITLE	ARTIST
2	8/03	14	1	1. Macarena (bayside boys mix)	Los Del Rio
30	5/18	8	1	2. Tha Crossroads	Bone thugs-n-harmony
52	3/23	6	1	3. Because You Loved Me	Celine Dion
329	5/04	2	1	4. Always Be My Baby	Mariah Carey
342	7/13	2	1	5. How Do U Want It	2 Pac (featuring KC & JoJo)
555	7/27	1	1	6. You're Makin' Me High	Toni Braxton
878	8/24	9	2	7. I Love You Always Forever	Donna Lewis
999	3/23	2	2	8. Nobody Knows	The Tony Rich Project
	3/09	2	2	9. Sittin' Up In My Room	Brandy featuring LL Cool J
	2/24	2	2	10. Not Gon' Cry	Mary J. Blige
	8/17	1	2	11. Twisted	Keith Sweat
	2/17	1	2	12. Missing	Everything But The Girl
	6/15	5	3	13. Give Me One Reason	Tracy Chapman
	8/17	1	3	14. C'Mon N' Ride It (The Train)	Quad City DJ's
	8/24	1	3	15. Loungin	L.L. Cool J
	8/31	1	3	16. Hit Me Off	New Edition
	4/13	5	4	17. Ironic	Alanis Morissette
	3/30	2	4	18. Down Low (Nobody Has To Know)	R. Kelly (featuring Ronald Isley & Ernie Isley)
	2/03	2	4	19. One Of Us	Joan Osborne
	8/17	2	5	20. Change The World	Eric Clapton
	4/27	2	5	21. 1,2,3,4 (Sumpin' New)	Coolio
	1/27	1	5	22. Name	Goo Goo Dolls
	8/03	1	5	23. I Can't Sleep Baby (If I)	R. Kelly
	6/08	1	5	24. You're The One	SWV (Sisters With Voices)
	1/20	1	5	25. Breakfast At Tiffany's	Deep Blue Something
	2/24	3	6	26. Be My Lover	La Bouche
	6/22	1	6	27. California Love	2 Pac (featuring Dr. Dre & Roger Troutman)
	7/27	1	6	28. You Learn	Alanis Morissette
	1/06	1	6	29. Free As A Bird	The Beatles
	6/22	2	7	30. Theme From Mission: Impossible	Adam Clayton & Larry Mullen
	2/24	2	7	31. Jesus To A Child	George Michael
	5/04	3	8	32. Count On Me	Whitney Houston & CeCe Winans
	4/20	2	8	33. WOO-HAH!! Got You All In Check	Busta Rhymes
	6/01	2	8	34. Fastlove	George Michael
	3/09	1	8	35. Wonderwall	Oasis
	3/09	4	9	36. Follow You Down	Gin Blossoms
	7/06	1	9	37. Why I Love You So Much	Monica
	4/13	1	9	38. Doin It	LL Cool J
	6/01	1	10	39. Keep On, Keepin' On	MC Lyte featuring Xscape
	3/30	1	10	40. Lady	D'Angelo

I HEARD IT THROUGH THE GRAPEVINE

By NORMAN WHITFIELD · BARRETT STRONG

Recorded by MARVIN GAYE on TAMLA T-54176

JOBETE MUSIC COMPANY, INC.

exclusive distributor Belwin Mills Publishing Corp.

95¢

JS 1018

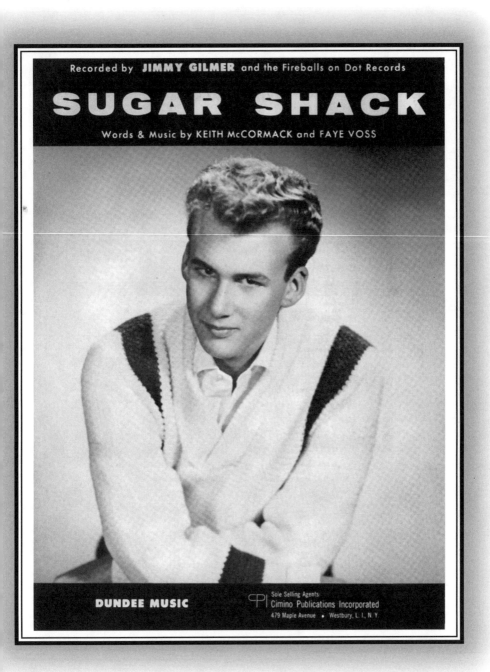

THE TOP
100 ALBUMS

This section displays, in rank order, the biggest #1 albums of *Billboard* magazine's pop albums charts from January 1, 1955 through December 28, 1996.

This ranking is based on the most weeks an album held the #1 position. Ties are broken according to this order: total weeks in the Top 10, total weeks in the Top 40, and finally, total weeks charted.

The total weeks at #1 and total weeks in the Top 10 are shown beside each album cover photo, along with the year the album peaked.

1.
"West Side Story"
Soundtrack

#1 – 54 Weeks
Top 10 Weeks: 106
Year: 1962

2.
"Thriller"
Michael Jacks

##1 – 37 Weeks
Top 10 Weeks:
Year: 1983

3.
"South Pacific"
Soundtrack

#1 – 31 Weeks
Top 10 Weeks: 90
Year: 1958

4.
"Calypso"
Harry Belafont

#1 – 31 Weeks
Top 10 Weeks:
Year: 1956

5.
"Rumours"
Fleetwood Mac

##1 – 31 Weeks
Top 10 Weeks: 52
Year: 1977

6.
"Saturday Night Feve"
**Bee Gees/
Soundtrack**

#1 – 24 Weeks
Top 10 Weeks:
Year: 1978

7.
"Purple Rain"
**Prince And The
Revolution/
Soundtrack**

#1 – 24 Weeks
Top 10 Weeks: 32
Year: 1984

8.
"Please Hammer D
Hurt 'Em"
M.C. Hammer

#1 – 21 Weeks
Top 10 Weeks:
Year: 1990

9.
"The Bodyguard"
**Whitney Houston/
Soundtrack**

#1 – 20 Weeks
Top 10 Weeks: 40
Year: 1992

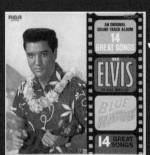

10.
"Blue Hawaii"
**Elvis Presley/
Soundtrack**

#1 – 20 Weeks
Top 10 Weeks: 39
Year: 1961

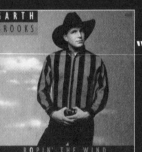

11.
"Ropin' The Wind"
Garth Brooks

#1 – 18 Weeks
Top 10 Weeks: 50
Year: 1991

12.
"Dirty Dancing"
Soundtrack

#1 – 18 Weeks
Top 10 Weeks: 48
Year: 1987

13.
"More Of The Monkees"
The Monkees

#1 – 18 Weeks
Top 10 Weeks: 25
Year: 1967

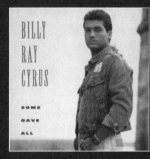

14.
"Some Gave All"
Billy Ray Cyrus

#1 – 17 Weeks
Top 10 Weeks: 43
Year: 1992

15.
"Synchronicity"
The Police

#1 – 17 Weeks
Top 10 Weeks: 40
Year: 1983

16.
"Love Me Or Leave Me"
**Doris Day/
Soundtrack**

#1 – 17 Weeks
Top 10 Weeks: 25
Year: 1955

17.
"The Sound Of Music"
Original Cast

#1 – 16 Weeks
Top 10 Weeks: 105
Year: 1960

18.
"To The Extreme"
Vanilla Ice

#1 – 16 Weeks
Top 10 Weeks: 2
Year: 1990

19.
"Days of Wine And Roses"
Andy Williams

#1 – 16 Weeks
Top 10 Weeks: 23
Year: 1963

20.
"My Fair La
Original Cast

#1 – 15 Weeks
Top 10 Weeks:
Year: 1956

21.
"Tapestry"
Carole King

#1 – 15 Weeks
Top 10 Weeks: 46
Year: 1971

22.
"Sgt. Peppe Lonely Hea Club Band"
The Beatles

#1 – 15 Weeks
Top 10 Weeks: 3
Year: 1967

23.
"Business As Usual"
Men At Work

#1 – 15 Weeks
Top 10 Weeks: 31
Year: 1982

24.
"The Kingston Trio At Large"
The Kingston Trio

#1 – 15 Weeks
Top 10 Weeks: 31
Year: 1959

25.
"Hi Infidelity"
REO Speedwagon

#1 – 15 Weeks
Top 10 Weeks: 30
Year: 1981

26.
"The Wall"
Pink Floyd

#1 – 15 Weeks
Top 10 Weeks: 27
Year: 1980

27.
"Mary Poppins"
Soundtrack

#1 – 14 Weeks
Top 10 Weeks: 48
Year: 1965

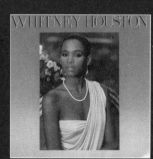

28.
"Whitney Houston"
Whitney Houston

#1 – 14 Weeks
Top 10 Weeks: 46
Year: 1986

29.
"The Button-Down Mind Of Bob Newhart"
Bob Newhart

#1 – 14 Weeks
Top 10 Weeks: 44
Year: 1960

30.
"Exodus"
Soundtrack

#1 – 14 Weeks
Top 10 Weeks: 38
Year: 1961

31.
"Songs In The Key Of Life"
Stevie Wonder

#1 –14 Weeks
Top 10 Weeks: 35
Year: 1976

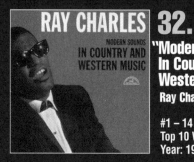

32.
"Modern Soun In Country A Western Mu
Ray Charles

#1 – 14 Weeks
Top 10 Weeks: 3:
Year: 1962

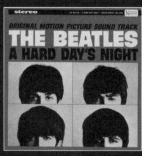

33.
"A Hard Day's Night"
The Beatles/ Soundtrack

#1 – 14 Weeks
Top 10 Weeks: 28
Year: 1964

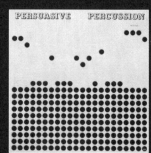

34.
"Persuasive Percussion"
Enoch Light/ Terry Snyder and The All-Star

#1 – 13 Weeks
Top 10 Weeks: 4:
Year: 1960

35.
"Judy At Carnegie Hall"
Judy Garland

#1 – 13 Weeks
Top 10 Weeks: 37
Year: 1961

36.
"The Monkee
The Monkees

#1 – 13 Weeks
Top 10 Weeks: 3:
Year: 1966

37.
"Hair"
Original Cast

#1 – 13 Weeks
Top 10 Weeks: 28
Year: 1969

38.
"Jagged Little Pill"*
Alanis Morissette

#1 – 12 Weeks
Top 10 Weeks: 69 ↑
Year: 1995

*Still in Top 10 as of December 28, 1996 cutoff date

39.
"The Music Man"
Original Cast

#1 – 12 Weeks
Top 10 Weeks: 66
Year: 1958

40.
"Faith"
George Michael

#1 – 12 Weeks
Top 10 Weeks: 51
Year: 1988

41.
"Breakfast At Tiffany's"
Henry Mancini/ Soundtrack

#1 –12 Weeks
Top 10 Weeks: 46
Year: 1962

42.
"Sold Out"
The Kingston Trio

#1 – 12 Weeks
Top 10 Weeks: 29
Year: 1960

43.
"Grease"
Soundtrack

#1 – 12 Weeks
Top 10 Weeks: 29
Year: 1978

44.
"The First Family"
Vaughn Meader

#1 – 12 Weeks
Top 10 Weeks: 17
Year: 1962

45.
"Mariah Carey"
Mariah Carey

#1 – 11 Weeks
Top 10 Weeks: 49
Year: 1991

46.
"Calcutta!"
Lawrence Welk

#1 – 11 Weeks
Top 10 Weeks: 3
Year: 1961

47.
"Whitney"
Whitney Houston

#1 – 11 Weeks
Top 10 Weeks: 31
Year: 1987

48.
"Abbey Road
The Beatles

#1 – 11 Weeks
Top 10 Weeks: 2
Year: 1969

49.
"Meet
The Beatles!"
The Beatles

#1 – 11 Weeks
Top 10 Weeks: 21
Year: 1964

50.
"Miami Vice"
TV Soundtrack

#1 – 11 Weeks
Top 10 Weeks: 1
Year: 1985

51.
"Forever Your Girl"
Paula Abdul

#1 –10 Weeks
Top 10 Weeks: 64
Year: 1989

52.
"Around The World In 80 Days"
Soundtrack

#1 – 10 Weeks
Top 10 Weeks: 54
Year: 1957

53.
"Gigi"
Soundtrack

#1 – 10 Weeks
Top 10 Weeks: 54
Year: 1958

54.
"Frampton Comes Alive!"
Peter Frampton

#1 – 10 Weeks
Top 10 Weeks: 52
Year: 1976

55.
"Elvis Presley"
Elvis Presley

#1 – 10 Weeks
Top 10 Weeks: 43
Year: 1956

56.
"The Music From Peter Gunn"
Henry Mancini

#1 – 10 Weeks
Top 10 Weeks: 43
Year: 1959

57.
"4"
Foreigner

#1 – 10 Weeks
Top 10 Weeks: 34
Year: 1981

58.
"The Lion Kin
Soundtrack

#1 – 10 Weeks
Top 10 Weeks: 3
Year: 1994

59.
"G.I. Blues"
Elvis Presley/
Soundtrack

#1 – 10 Weeks
Top 10 Weeks: 29
Year: 1960

60.
"Footloose"
Soundtrack

#1 – 10 Weeks
Top 10 Weeks: 2
Year: 1984

61.
"String Along"
The Kingston Trio

#1 –10 Weeks
Top 10 Weeks: 20
Year: 1960

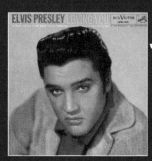

62.
"Loving You'
Elvis Presley/
Soundtrack

#1 – 10 Weeks
Top 10 Weeks: 1
Year: 1957

63.
"The Singing Nun"
The Singing Nun

#1 – 10 Weeks
Top 10 Weeks: 18
Year: 1963

64.
"Bridge Over Troubled Water"
Simon and Garf

#1 – 10 Weeks
Top 10 Weeks: 1
Year: 1970

65.
"Elton John - Greatest Hits"
Elton John

#1 – 10 Weeks
Top 10 Weeks: 11
Year: 1974

66.
"Brothers In Arms"
Dire Straits

#1 – 9 Weeks
Top 10 Weeks: 37
Year: 1985

67.
"The Joshua Tree"
U2

#1 – 9 Weeks
Top 10 Weeks: 35
Year: 1987

68.
"What Now My Love"
Herb Alpert & the Tijuana Brass

#1 – 9 Weeks
Top 10 Weeks: 32
Year: 1966

69.
"Asia"
Asia

#1 – 9 Weeks
Top 10 Weeks: 27
Year: 1982

70.
"The Graduate"
Simon & Garfunkel/ Soundtrack

#1 – 9 Weeks
Top 10 Weeks: 26
Year: 1968

71.
"American Fool"
John Cougar

#1 – 9 Weeks
Top 10 Weeks: 22
Year: 1982

72.
"Tatoo You"
The Rolling Stones

#1 – 9 Weeks
Top 10 Weeks: 22
Year: 1981

73.
"Stars For A Summer Night"
Various Artists

#1 – 9 Weeks
Top 10 Weeks: 21
Year: 1961

74.
"The Long R
Eagles

#1 – 9 Weeks
Top 10 Weeks: 2
Year: 1979

75.
"Nice 'n' Easy"
Frank Sinatra

#1 – 9 Weeks
Top 10 Weeks: 19
Year: 1960

76.
"Cosmo's Factory"
Creedence Clearwater Re

#1 – 9 Weeks
Top 10 Weeks: 1
Year: 1970

77.
"Beatles '65"
The Beatles

#1 – 9 Weeks
Top 10 Weeks: 16
Year: 1965

78.
"Help!"
The Beatles/ Soundtrack

#1 – 9 Weeks
Top 10 Weeks: 1
Year: 1965

79.
"The Beatles [White Album]"
The Beatles

#1 – 9 Weeks
Top 10 Weeks: 15
Year: 1968

80.
"Pearl"
Janis Joplin

#1 – 9 Weeks
Top 10 Weeks: 15
Year: 1971

81.
"Chicago V"
Chicago

#1 – 9 Weeks
Top 10 Weeks: 13
Year: 1972

82.
"Whipped Cream & Other Delights"
Herb Alpert's Tijuana Brass

#1 – 8 Weeks
Top 10 Weeks: 61
Year: 1965

83.
"Cracked Rear View"
Hootie & The Blowfish

#1 – 8 Weeks
Top 10 Weeks: 55
Year: 1995

84.
"Sing Along With Mitch"
Mitch Miller & The Gang

#1 – 8 Weeks
Top 10 Weeks: 53
Year: 1958

85.
"Slippery When Wet"
Bon Jovi

#1 – 8 Weeks
Top 10 Weeks: 46
Year: 1986

86.
"Girl You Kn It's True"
Milli Vanilli

#1 – 8 Weeks
Top 10 Weeks: 4
Year: 1989

87.
"Goodbye Yellow Brick Road"
Elton John

#1 – 8 Weeks
Top 10 Weeks: 36
Year: 1973

88.
"Music Box"
Mariah Carey

#1 – 8 Weeks
Top 10 Weeks: 3
Year: 1993

89.
"Love Is The Thing"
Nat "King" Cole

#1 – 8 Weeks
Top 10 Weeks: 31
Year: 1957

90.
"Hotel California"
Eagles

#1 – 8 Weeks
Top 10 Weeks: 2
Year: 1977

91.
"Here We Go Again!"
The Kingston Trio

#1 – 8 Weeks
Top 10 Weeks: 26
Year: 1959

92.
"Double Fantasy"
John Lennon/ Yoko Ono

#1 – 8 Weeks
Top 10 Weeks:
Year: 1980

93.
"52nd Street"
Billy Joel

#1 – 8 Weeks
Top 10 Weeks: 22
Year: 1978

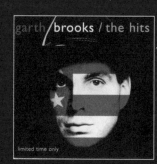

94.
"The Hits"
Garth Brooks

#1 – 8 Weeks
Top 10 Weeks: 20
Year: 1995

95.
"Cheap Thrills"
**Big Brother And the
Holding Company**

#1 – 8 Weeks
Top 10 Weeks: 19
Year: 1968

96.
"Magical
Mystery Tour"
The Beatles

#1 – 8 Weeks
Top 10 Weeks: 14
Year: 1968

97.
"My Son,
The Nut"
Allan Sherman

#1 – 8 Weeks
Top 10 Weeks: 12
Year: 1963

98.
"Peter, Paul
and Mary"
**Peter, Paul
and Mary**

#1 – 7 Weeks
Top 10 Weeks: 85
Year: 1962

99.
"Born In
The U.S.A."
Bruce Springsteen

#1 – 7 Weeks
Top 10 Weeks: 84
Year: 1984

100.
"Blood, Sweat
& Tears"
**Blood, Sweat
& Tears**

#1 – 7 Weeks
Top 10 Weeks: 50
Year: 1969

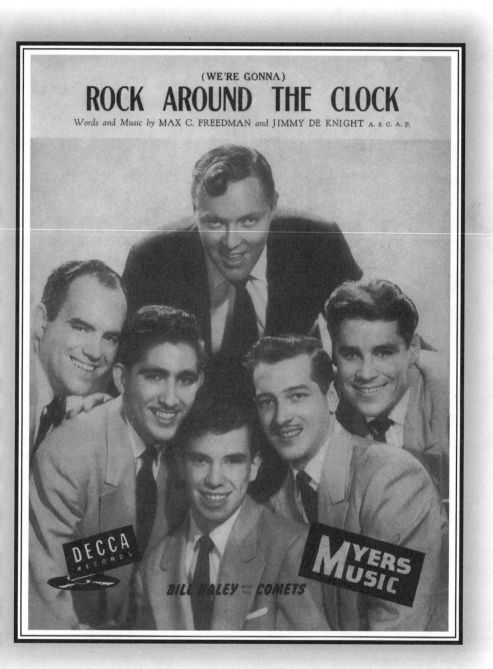

THE ARTISTS

This section lists, alphabetically by artist name, every single listed in the Top 1000 ranking.

Each artist's hits are listed in rank order, with the Top 1000 ranking next to each title, along with the original label and number. This makes for a handy guide in quickly viewing each artist's all-time greatest hits.

A

ABBA
644 Dancing Queen ....Atlantic 3372

ABBOTT, Gregory
639 Shake You Down ....Columbia 06191

ABDUL, Paula
109 Rush, Rush ....Virgin 98828
290 Straight Up ....Virgin 99256
294 Opposites Attract ....Virgin 99158
Paula Abdul With The Wild Pair
507 Forever Your Girl ....Virgin 99230
647 Cold Hearted............................Virgin 99196
854 The Promise Of A New Day ....Virgin 98752

ACE OF BASE
51 The Sign ....Arista 12653
922 All That She Wants ....Arista 12614

ADAMS, Bryan
49 (Everything I Do) I Do It For You....A&M 1567
88 Have You Ever Really
Loved A Woman? ....A&M 1028
205 All For Love ....A&M 0476
Bryan Adams/Rod Stewart/Sting
515 Heaven ....A&M 2729

A-HA
686 Take On Me............................Warner 29011

AIR SUPPLY
664 The One That You Love............Arista 0604
904 All Out Of Love ....Arista 0520
949 Making Love Out Of
Nothing At All ....Arista 9056

ALL-4-ONE
8 I Swear..................................Blitzz/Atl. 87243

ALPERT, Herb
189 This Guy's In Love With You ....A&M 929
380 Rise ....A&M 2151

AMERICA
239 A Horse With No Name ....Warner 7555
873 Sister Golden Hair ....Warner 8086

ANGELS, The
255 My Boyfriend's Back ....Smash 1834

ANIMALS, The
287 The House Of The Rising Sun....MGM 13264

ANKA, Paul
156 Lonely Boy ....ABC-Para. 10022
323 (You're) Having My Baby.......United Art. 454
568 Diana ....ABC-Para. 9831
939 Put Your Head On
My Shoulder....................ABC-Para. 10040

ARCHIES, The
136 Sugar, Sugar ....Calendar 1008

ARMSTRONG, Louis
564 Hello, Dolly! ....Kapp 573

ASSOCIATION, The
172 Windy.....................................Warner 7041
321 Cherish ....Valiant 747

ASTLEY, Rick
463 Never Gonna Give You Up.........RCA 5347
820 Together Forever........................RCA 8319

ATLANTIC STARR
702 Always...................................Warner 28455

AUSTIN, Patti, with James Ingram
366 Baby, Come To Me ....Qwest 50036

AVALON, Frankie
103 Venus................................Chancellor 1031
629 Why ....Chancellor 1045

AWB (AVERAGE WHITE BAND)
731 Pick Up The Pieces ....Atlantic 3229

B

BACHMAN-TURNER OVERDRIVE
856 You Ain't Seen Nothing Yet ...Mercury 73622

BAD ENGLISH
503 When I See You Smile..............Epic 69082

BANANARAMA
737 Venus ....London 886056

BANGLES
181 Walk Like An Egyptian ....Columbia 06257
796 Eternal Flame.....................Columbia 68533

BASIL, Toni
580 Mickey ....Chrysalis 2638

BAXTER, Les
56 The Poor People Of Paris ....Capitol 3336
326 Unchained Melody ....Capitol 3055

BAY CITY ROLLERS
821 Saturday Night..........................Arista 0149

BEACH BOYS, The
393 I Get Around ....Capitol 5174
488 Help Me, Rhonda....................Capitol 5395
749 Good Vibrations ....Capitol 5676
844 Kokomo.................................Elektra 69385

BEATLES, The
17 Hey Jude ....Apple 2276
45 I Want To Hold Your Hand ....Capitol 5112
115 Get Back....................................Apple 2490
118 Can't Buy Me Love...................Capitol 5150
196 Yesterday ....Capitol 5498
286 Hello Goodbye ....Capitol 2056
313 We Can Work It Out................Capitol 5555
315 I Feel Fine...............................Capitol 5327
322 Help!.......................................Capitol 5476
351 She Loves You ....Swan 4152
352 Let It Be ....Apple 2764
446 A Hard Day's Night ....Capitol 5222
545 The Long And Winding Road ....Apple 2832
553 Paperback Writer ....Capitol 5651
554 Eight Days A Week ....Capitol 5371

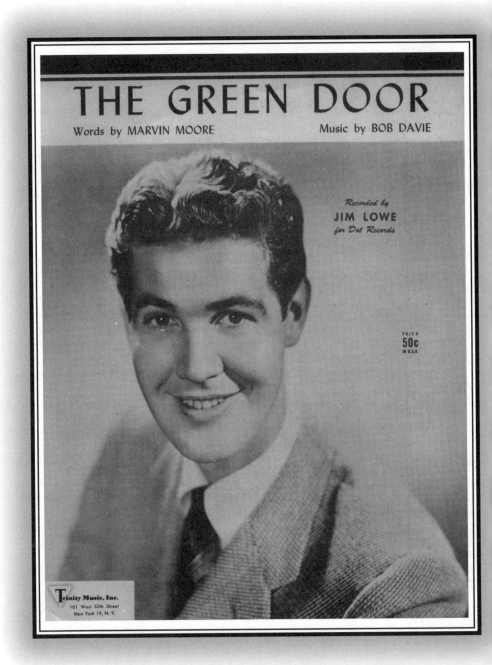

C

CAMPBELL, Glen
369 Rhinestone Cowboy ....Capitol 4095
649 Southern Nights ....Capitol 4376

C & C MUSIC FACTORY
371 Gonna Make You Sweat
    (Everybody Dance Now) ..Columbia 73604

CAPTAIN & TENNILLE
194 Love Will Keep Us Together........A&M 1672
560 Do That To Me One
    More Time ....Casablanca 2215

CARA, Irene
61 Flashdance...
    What A Feeling ....Casablanca 811440

CAREY, Mariah
1 One Sweet Day ....Columbia 78074
    Mariah Carey & Boyz II Men
21 Fantasy ....Columbia 78043
25 Dreamlover ....Columbia 77080
123 Hero..................................Columbia 77224
191 Vision Of Love ....Columbia 73348
288 Emotions...........................Columbia 73977
289 Love Takes Time.................Columbia 73455
329 Always Be My Baby.............Columbia 78276
429 I'll Be There........................Columbia 74330
432 I Don't Wanna Cry ....Columbia 73743
462 Someday.............................Columbia 73561

CARLISLE, Belinda
778 Heaven Is A Place On Earth.....MCA 53181

CARMEN, Eric
980 All By Myself..............................Arista 0165

CARNES, Kim
16 Bette Davis Eyes...............EMI America 8077

CARPENTERS
144 (They Long To Be) Close To You ...A&M 1183
416 Top Of The World.......................A&M 1468
857 Please Mr. Postman..................A&M 1646
911 We've Only Just Begun ....A&M 1217

CASH, Johnny
975 A Boy Named Sue ....Columbia 44944

CASSIDY, Shaun
735 Da Doo Ron Ron ....Warner/Curb 8365

CETERA, Peter
509 Glory Of Love....................Full Moon 28662
780 The Next Time I Fall............Full Moon 28597
    Peter Cetera w/Amy Grant

CHAMPS, The
93 Tequila ....Challenge 1016

CHANDLER, Gene
280 Duke Of Earl............................Vee-Jay 416

CHANNEL, Bruce
278 Hey! Baby................................Smash 1731

CHAPIN, Harry
819 Cat's In The Cradle.................Elektra 45203

CHARLES, Ray
97 I Can't Stop Loving You ......ABC-Para. 10330
448 Hit The Road Jack..............ABC-Para. 10244
864 Georgia On My Mind.........ABC-Para. 10135

CHEAP TRICK
505 The Flame.................................Epic 07745

CHECKER, Chubby
197 The Twist...............................Parkway 811
264 Pony Time ....Parkway 818

CHER
386 Gypsys, Tramps & Thieves.........Kapp 2146
428 Half-Breed ....MCA 40102
826 Dark Lady...............................MCA 40161

CHIC
58 Le Freak...............................Atlantic 3519
623 Good Times ....Atlantic 3584

CHICAGO
340 Hard To Say I'm Sorry.........Full Moon 29979
375 If You Leave Me Now..........Columbia 10390
413 Look Away ....Reprise 27766

CHIFFONS, The
175 He's So Fine ....Laurie 3152

CHILD, Jane
979 Don't Wanna Fall In Love ....Warner 19933

CHI-LITES, The
718 Oh Girl ....Brunswick 55471

CHIPMUNKS, The
195 The Chipmunk Song..............Liberty 55168

CHRISTIE, Lou
837 Lightnin' Strikes ....MGM 13412

CLAPTON, Eric
863 I Shot The Sheriff ....RSO 409
898 Tears In Heaven....................Reprise 19038

CLARK, Dave, Five
836 Over And Over ....Epic 9863

CLARK, Petula
395 Downtown ....Warner 5494
547 My Love ....Warner 5684

CLUB NOUVEAU
534 Lean On Me....................King Jay/War. 28430

COASTERS, The
619 Yakety Yak ....Atco 6116
965 Charlie Brown ....Atco 6132

COCKER, Joe, and Jennifer Warnes
292 Up Where We Belong ....Island 99996

COLLINS, Phil
154 Another Day In Paradise ....Atlantic 8877
229 Against All Odds
    (Take A Look At Me Now)...Atlantic 89700
475 Two Hearts ....Atlantic 8898
519 Groovy Kind Of Love.............Atlantic 8901
531 One More Night......................Atlantic 8958
608 Separate Lives ....Atlantic 8949
    Phil Collins and Marilyn Martin
798 Sussudio ....Atlantic 8956

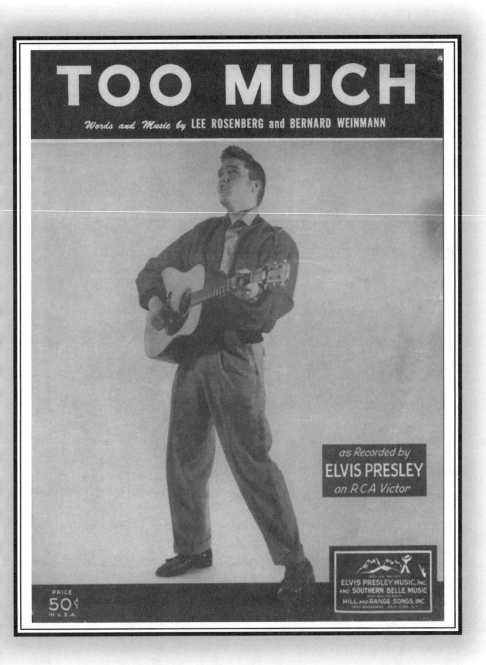

J

JACKS, Terry
258 Seasons In The Sun ....Bell 45432

JACKSON, Janet
26 That's The Way Love Goes ......Virgin 12650
184 Miss You Much.............................A&M 1445
263 Escapade....................................A&M 1490
332 Again ....Virgin 38404
523 When I Think Of You ....A&M 2855
690 Love Will Never Do
(Without You) ....A&M 1538
859 Black Cat ....A&M 1477

JACKSON, Michael
47 Billie Jean ....Epic 03509
50 Black Or White...........................Epic 74100
64 Say Say Say ....Columbia 04168
Paul McCartney And Michael Jackson
162 Rock With You ....Epic 50797
226 Beat It ....Epic 03759
477 Man In The Mirror ....Epic 07668
550 Bad ....Epic 07418
588 You Are Not Alone ....Epic 78002
754 Ben...Motown 1207
807 The Way You Make Me Feel ......Epic 07645
818 Don't Stop 'Til You Get Enough ...Epic 50742
835 I Just Can't Stop Loving You ......Epic 07253
860 Dirty Diana.................................Epic 07739
946 The Girl Is Mine ....Epic 03288
Michael Jackson/Paul McCartney

JACKSON 5
94 I'll Be There ....Motown 1171
404 ABC...Motown 1163
405 The Love You Save ....Motown 1166
611 I Want You Back ....Motown 1157
976 Never Can Say Goodbye ....Motown 1179

JAMES, Sonny
566 Young Love...............................Capitol 3602

JAMES, Tommy, And The Shondells
348 Crimson And Clover ....Roulette 7028
544 Hanky Panky ....Roulette 4686
956 Crystal Blue Persuasion ....Roulette 7050

JAN & DEAN
490 Surf City ....Liberty 55580

JEFFERSON STARSHIP - see STARSHIP

JETT, Joan, & The Blackhearts
43 I Love Rock 'N Roll ....Boardwalk 135

JOEL, Billy
343 It's Still Rock And
Roll To Me ....Columbia 11276
423 We Didn't Start The Fire ......Columbia 73021
697 Tell Her About It..................Columbia 04012

JOHN, Elton
148 That's What Friends Are For......Arista 9422
Dionne & Friends
182 Don't Go Breaking My Heart ..Rocket 40585
Elton John and Kiki Dee
247 Crocodile Rock..........................MCA 40000
306 Island Girl.................................MCA 40461
374 Philadelphia Freedom ....MCA 40364
The Elton John Band
541 Lucy In The Sky
With Diamonds ....MCA 40344
612 Bennie And The Jets.................MCA 40198
641 Don't Let The Sun Go
Down On Me ....Columbia 74086
George Michael/Elton John
969 Goodbye Yellow Brick Road ......MCA 40148

JOHN, Robert
596 Sad Eyes.........................EMI America 8015

JOHNNY HATES JAZZ
983 Shattered Dreams...................Virgin 99383

JOPLIN, Janis
443 Me And Bobby McGee ....Columbia 45314

JORDAN, Montell
37 This Is How We Do It.........PMP/RAL 851468

JOURNEY
887 Open Arms ....Columbia 02687

K

KAEMPFERT, Bert
233 Wonderland By Night ....Decca 31141

KAMOZE, Ini
330 Here Comes
The Hotstepper ....Columbia 77614

KC And The SUNSHINE BAND
392 That's The Way (I Like It) ............T.K. 1015
573 Please Don't Go.........................T.K. 1035
575 (Shake, Shake, Shake)
Shake Your Booty....................T.K. 1019
772 I'm Your Boogie Man ...................T.K. 1022
874 Get Down Tonight.......................T.K. 1009
968 Keep It Comin' Love....................T.K. 1023

K-DOE, Ernie
674 Mother-In-Law ....Minit 623

KELLY, R.
132 Bump N' Grind...........................Jive 42207

KENDRICKS, Eddie
359 Keep On Truckin' (Part 1)........Tamla 54238

KENNER, Chris
977 I Like It Like That, Part 1 ....Instant 3229

KIM, Andy
805 Rock Me Gently ....Capitol 3895

KING, Carole
102 It's Too Late...............................Ode 66015

KINGSMEN, The
889 Louie Louie ....Wand 143

Recorded by THE SHIRELLES on SCEPTER Records

Will You Love Me Tomorrow

By GERRY GOFFIN and CAROLE KING

ALDON MUSIC, INC.   NEVINS-KIRSHNER ASSOCIATES, INC.   60¢

Sole Selling Agents: KEYS-HANSEN, INC. 119 W. 57th ST. NEW YORK 19 N.Y.

KINGSTON TRIO, The
569 Tom Dooley ....Capitol 4049

KNACK, The
70 My Sharona.............................Capitol 4731

KNIGHT, Gladys, & The Pips
148 That's What Friends Are For......Arista 9422
       Dionne & Friends
417 Midnight Train To Georgia ....Buddah 383
954 I Heard It Through
       The Grapevine.......................Soul 35039

KNOX, Buddy
586 Party Doll..............................Roulette 4002

KOOL & THE GANG
453 Celebration ....De-Lite 807
967 Cherish ....De-Lite 880869

KRIS KROSS
28 Jump ....Ruffhouse 74197

L

LaBELLE
729 Lady Marmalade.......................Epic 50048

LaBELLE, Patti, And
Michael McDonald
293 On My Own..............................MCA 52770

LAUPER, Cyndi
382 Time After Time.....................Portrait 04432
530 True Colors ....Portrait 06247

LAWRENCE, Steve
402 Go Away Little Girl..............Columbia 42601

LAWRENCE, Vicki
468 The Night The Lights
       Went Out In Georgia ....Bell 45303

LEE, Brenda
217 I'm Sorry................................Decca 31093
813 I Want To Be Wanted..............Decca 31149

LEMON PIPERS, The
752 Green Tambourine.....................Buddah 23

LENNON, John
85 (Just Like) Starting Over ....Geffen 49604
876 Whatever Gets You
       Thru The Night ....Apple 1874
933 Woman...................................Geffen 49644

LEWIS, Bobby
42 Tossin' And Turnin'..................Beltone 1002

LEWIS, Donna
878 I Love You Always Forever .....Atlantic 87072

LEWIS, Gary, And The Playboys
409 This Diamond Ring.................Liberty 55756

LEWIS, Huey, and the News
301 Stuck With You ....Chrysalis 43019
422 The Power Of Love ....Chrysalis 42876
829 Jacob's Ladder....................Chrysalis 43097

LEWIS, Jerry Lee
912 Great Balls Of Fire ....Sun 281

LIGHTFOOT, Gordon
753 Sundown ....Reprise 1194

LIPPS, INC.
165 Funkytown ....Casablanca 2233

LISA LISA AND CULT JAM
708 Head To Toe......................Columbia 07008
804 Lost In Emotion ....Columbia 07267

LITTLE EVA
741 The Loco-Motion..................Dimension 1000

LOEB, Lisa, & Nine Stories
201 Stay (I Missed You)...................RCA 62870

LOGGINS, Kenny
219 Footloose ....Columbia 04310

LONDON, Laurie
170 He's Got The Whole World
       (In His Hands).......................Capitol 3891

LONDONBEAT
794 I've Been Thinking
       About You.......................Radioactive 54005

LOOKING GLASS
591 Brandy (You're A Fine Girl)........Epic 10874

LOS DEL RIO
2 Macarena (bayside boys mix) ...RCA 64407

LOS LOBOS
295 La Bamba...............................Slash 28336

LOVE UNLIMITED ORCHESTRA
683 Love's Theme...................20th Century 2069

LOVIN' SPOONFUL, The
317 Summer In The City............Kama Sutra 211

LOWE, Jim
199 The Green Door.......................Dot 15486

LULU
110 To Sir With Love.......................Epic 10187

L.V. - see COOLIO

M

M
595 Pop Muzik...................................Sire 49033

MacGREGOR, Mary
356 Torn Between Two Lovers ....Ariola Am. 7638

MADDOX, Johnny
882 The Crazy Otto ....Dot 15325

MADONNA
34 Take A Bow....................Maverick/Sire 18000
78 Like A Virgin ....Sire 29210
257 Vogue ....Sire 19863
305 Like A Prayer...........................Sire 27539
436 Justify My Love ....Sire 19485
474 Papa Don't Preach ....Sire 28660
621 Crazy For You.........................Geffen 29051
660 This Used To Be My Playground...Sire 18822
797 Open Your Heart.......................Sire 28508

O

OCEAN, Billy
456   Caribbean Queen
      (No More Love On The Run)....Jive 9199
469   Get Outta My Dreams,
      Get Into My Car ....Jive 9678
704   There'll Be Sad Songs
      (To Make You Cry) ....Jive 9465

O'CONNOR, Sinéad
152   Nothing Compares 2 U ....Ensign 23488

O'DAY, Alan
681   Undercover Angel ....Pacific 001

OHIO PLAYERS
592   Love Rollercoaster ....Mercury 73734
872   Fire ....Mercury 73643

O'JAYS, The
815   Love Train...............................Phil. Int. 3524

ORBISON, Roy
266   Oh, Pretty Woman................Monument 851
870   Running Scared ....Monument 438

ORLANDO, Tony - see DAWN

OSMOND, Donny
250   Go Away Little Girl....................MGM 14285

OSMONDS, The
114   One Bad Apple ....MGM 14193

O'SULLIVAN, Gilbert
73   Alone Again (Naturally) ....MAM 3619

P

PAGE, Tommy
853   I'll Be Your Everything................Sire 19959

PALMER, Robert
701   Addicted To Love ....Island 99570

PAPER LACE
832   The Night Chicago Died........Mercury 73492

PARKER, Ray Jr.
235   Ghostbusters ....Arista 9212

PARR, John
466   St. Elmo's Fire
      (Man In Motion)..................Atlantic 89541

PARTON, Dolly
339   Islands In The Stream ....RCA 13615
    Kenny Rogers with Dolly Parton
368   9 To 5 ....RCA 12133

PARTRIDGE FAMILY, The
221   I Think I Love You ....Bell 910

PAUL, Billy
265   Me And Mrs. Jones ....Phil. Int. 3521

PAUL & PAULA
254   Hey Paula...............................Philips 40084

PEACHES & HERB
151   Reunited................................Polydor 14547

PERKINS, Carl
901   Blue Suede Shoes ....Sun 234

PETER AND GORDON
678   A World Without Love..............Capitol 5175

PETER, PAUL & MARY
587   Leaving On A Jet Plane...........Warner 7340

PET SHOP BOYS
706   West End Girls.................EMI America 8307

PICKETT, Bobby "Boris",
And The Crypt-Kickers
411   Monster Mash ....Garpax 44167

PINK FLOYD
134   Another Brick In The Wall
      (Part II) ....Columbia 11187

PLATTERS, The
84   My Prayer ....Mercury 70893
231   Smoke Gets In Your Eyes .....Mercury 71383
336   The Great Pretender ....Mercury 70753
572   Twilight Time.........................Mercury 71289

PLAYER
228   Baby Come Back ....RSO 879

PM DAWN
634   Set Adrift On Memory Bliss..Gee St. 866094

POINTER SISTERS
937   Slow Hand ....Planet 47929

POISON
261   Every Rose Has Its Thorn .....Enigma 44203

POLICE, The
27   Every Breath You Take................A&M 2542

PRADO, Perez
9   Cherry Pink And Apple
      Blossom White........................RCA 5965
558   Patricia ....RCA 7245

PRESLEY, Elvis
6   Don't Be Cruel ....RCA 47-6604
7   Hound Dog...............................RCA 47-6604
15   All Shook Up ....RCA 47-6870
24   Heartbreak Hotel.....................RCA 47-6420
36   Jailhouse Rock........................RCA 47-7035
38   (Let Me Be Your) Teddy Bear ..RCA 47-7000
75   Are You Lonesome To-night? ..RCA 47-7810
83   Love Me Tender ....RCA 47-6643
92   It's Now Or Never....................RCA 47-7777
98   Don't.....................................RCA 47-7150
158   Stuck On You ....RCA 47-7740
248   Too Much ....RCA 47-6800
450   Surrender ....RCA 47-7850
489   Good Luck Charm...................RCA 47-7992
495   A Big Hunk O' Love ....RCA 47-7600
517   Hard Headed Woman ....RCA 47-7280
563   I Want You, I Need You,
      I Love You ....RCA 47-6540
814   Suspicious Minds ....RCA 47-9764
891   Return To Sender...................RCA 47-8100

PRESTON, Billy
427 Will It Go Round In Circles ....A&M 1411
713 Nothing From Nothing ....A&M 1544

PRESTON, Johnny
234 Running Bear ....Mercury 71474

PRICE, Lloyd
153 Stagger Lee ....ABC-Para. 9972
945 Personality ....ABC-Para. 10018

PRIEST, Maxi
680 Close To You ....Charisma 98951

PRINCE
91 When Doves Cry ....Warner 29286
384 Let's Go Crazy ....Warner 29216
455 Cream ....Paisley P. 19175
473 Kiss ....Paisley P. 28751
831 Batdance ....Warner 22924

PUCKETT, Gary - see UNION GAP

Q

QUEEN
139 Crazy Little Thing Called Love...Elektra 46579
204 Another One Bites The Dust ..Elektra 47031

? (QUESTION MARK) &
THE MYSTERIANS
630 96 Tears...................................Cameo 428

R

RABBITT, Eddie
367 I Love A Rainy Night...............Elektra 47066

RAFFERTY, Gerry
888 Baker Street........................United Art. 1192

RAIDERS
615 Indian Reservation
(The Lament Of The Cherokee
Reservation Indian) ....Columbia 45332

RASCALS - see YOUNG RASCALS
READY FOR THE WORLD
801 Oh Sheila ....MCA 52636

REDDING, Otis
145 (Sittin' On) The Dock Of The Bay ..Volt 157

REDDY, Helen
656 I Am Woman ....Capitol 3350
661 Delta Dawn............................Capitol 3645
808 Angie Baby............................Capitol 3972

REEVES, Jim
931 He'll Have To Go ....RCA 7643

REO SPEEDWAGON
262 Can't Fight This Feeling............Epic 04713
594 Keep On Loving You ....Epic 50953

REVERE, Paul - see RAIDERS

REYNOLDS, Debbie
80 Tammy ....Coral 61851

RHYTHM HERITAGE
816 Theme From S.W.A.T. ....ABC 12135

RICH, Charlie
500 The Most Beautiful Girl.............Epic 11040

RICH, Tony, Project
999 Nobody Knows ....LaFace 24115

RICHIE, Lionel
18 Endless Love..........................Motown 1519
Diana Ross & Lionel Richie
130 All Night Long (All Night)........Motown 1698
164 Say You, Say Me ....Motown 1819
353 Hello ....Motown 1722
364 Truly....................................Motown 1644

RIDDLE, Nelson
121 Lisbon Antigua ....Capitol 3287

RIGHTEOUS BROTHERS, The
284 (You're My) Soul
And Inspiration ....Verve 10383
391 You've Lost That Lovin' Feelin' ...Philles 124

RIGHT SAID FRED
215 I'm Too Sexy ....Charisma 98671

RILEY, Jeannie C.
632 Harper Valley P.T.A...................Plantation 3

RIPERTON, Minnie
668 Lovin' You ....Epic 50057

RIVERS, Johnny
745 Poor Side Of Town................Imperial 66205

ROBBINS, Marty
379 El Paso ....Columbia 41511

ROBINSON, Smokey
944 Being With You ....Tamla 54321

ROCKWELL
960 Somebody's Watching Me.......Motown 1702

RODGERS, Jimmie
127 Honeycomb ....Roulette 4015

ROE, Tommy
171 Dizzy.....................................ABC 11164
538 Sheila ....ABC-Para. 10329

ROGERS, Kenny
63 Lady.....................................Liberty 1380
339 Islands In The Stream ....RCA 13615
Kenny Rogers with Dolly Parton

ROLLING STONES, The
146 Honky Tonk Women ....London 910
176 (I Can't Get No) Satisfaction....London 9766
447 Brown Sugar.......................Rolling S. 19100
499 Paint It, Black ....London 901
540 Get Off Of My Cloud...............London 9792
610 Miss You..............................Rolling S. 19307
733 Angie ....Rolling S. 19105
768 Ruby Tuesday........................London 904
935 Start Me Up ....Rolling S. 21003
992 19th Nervous Breakdown ....London 9823

SINATRA, Nancy
179   Somethin' Stupid ....Reprise 0561
      Nancy Sinatra & Frank Sinatra
748   These Boots Are Made
      For Walkin' ....Reprise 0432

SINGING NUN, The
177   Dominique ....Philips 40152

SIR MIX-A-LOT
82   Baby Got Back ....Def Amer. 18947

SLEDGE, Percy
542   When A Man Loves
      A Woman..............................Atlantic 2326

SLY & THE FAMILY STONE
168   Everyday People.......................Epic 10407
251   Family Affair..............................Epic 10805
486   Thank You (Falettinme
      Be Mice Elf Agin)...................Epic 10555

SMYTH, Patty, with Don Henley
886   Sometimes Love Just
      Ain't Enough ....MCA 54403

SNOW
39   Informer ....EastWest 98471

SONNY & CHER
316   I Got You Babe ....Atco 6359

SOUL, David
724   Don't Give Up On Us...........Private S. 45129

SOUL, Jimmy
539   If You Wanna Be Happy.........S.P.Q.R. 3305

SOUL FOR REAL
899   Candy Rain ....Uptown/MCA 54906

SPINNERS
652   Then Came You ....Atlantic 3202
      Dionne Warwicke And Spinners
950   The Rubberband Man.............Atlantic 3355

SPRINGFIELD, Rick
338   Jessie's Girl...............................RCA 12201
902   Don't Talk To Strangers ....RCA 13070

SPRINGSTEEN, Bruce
909   Dancing In The Dark...........Columbia 04463

STAPLE SINGERS, The
665   I'll Take You There ....Stax 0125
744   Let's Do It Again ....Curtom 0109

STARLAND VOCAL BAND
431   Afternoon Delight ....Windsong 10588

STARR, Edwin
273   War...Gordy 7101

STARR, Kay
55   Rock And Roll Waltz ....RCA 6359

STARR, Ringo
743   You're Sixteen.............................Apple 1870
825   Photograph ....Apple 1865

STARSHIP
420   Nothing's Gonna Stop Us Now..Grunt 5109
457   We Built This City....................Grunt 14170
723   Sara...Grunt 14253

STARS on 45
657   Medley ....Radio 3810

STEAM
434   Na Na Hey Hey
      Kiss Him Goodbye..............Fontana 1667

STEPPENWOLF
986   Born To Be Wild ....Dunhill 4138

STEVENS, Ray
276   The Streak.............................Barnaby 600
528   Everything Is Beautiful ....Barnaby 2011

STEVIE B
150   Because I Love You
      (The Postman Song) ....LMR 2724

STEWART, Amii
790   Knock On Wood ....Ariola Am. 7736

STEWART, Rod
31   Tonight's The Night
      (Gonna Be Alright) ....Warner 8262
96   Maggie May..........................Mercury 73224
137   Da Ya Think I'm Sexy? ....Warner 8724
205   All For Love................................A&M 0476
      Bryan Adams/Rod Stewart/Sting

STING - see ADAMS, Bryan

STOLOFF, Morris
203   Moonglow and Theme
      From "Picnic".......................Decca 29888

STORIES
424   Brother Louie ....Kama Sutra 577

STORM, Gale
928   I Hear You Knocking ....Dot 15412

STRAWBERRY ALARM CLOCK
624   Incense And Peppermints...........Uni 55018

STREISAND, Barbra
208   Love Theme From "A Star Is Born"
      (Evergreen)......................Columbia 10450
216   Woman In Love....................Columbia 11364
241   The Way We Were..............Columbia 45944
360   You Don't Bring Me Flowers...Columbia 10840
      Barbra Streisand & Neil Diamond
399   No More Tears
      (Enough Is Enough) ....Columbia 11125
      Barbra Streisand/Donna Summer

STYX
350   Babe ....A&M 2188

SUMMER, Donna
100   Bad Girls ....Casablanca 988
207   Hot Stuff.............................Casablanca 978
244   MacArthur Park...................Casablanca 939
399   No More Tears
      (Enough Is Enough) ....Columbia 11125
      Barbra Streisand/Donna Summer

SUPREMES, The
190   Baby Love ....Motown 1066
347   Love Child ....Motown 1135
400   Come See About Me ....Motown 1068
401   Where Did Our Love Go ....Motown 1060
449   You Can't Hurry Love ....Motown 1097

T

U

Y

Z

THE SONGS

This section lists, alphabetically, all titles listed in the Top 1000 ranking. Listed next to each title is its final ranking in the Top 1000.

A song with more than one charted version is listed once, with the artist's names listed below it in rank order. Songs that have the same title, but are different tunes, are listed separately, with the highest-ranked song listed first.

A

B

M

T

Recorded By **THE TEMPTATIONS** on Gordy Records

MY GIRL

By **WILLIAM ROBINSON** and **RONALD WHITE**

Jan. 10 Chart

JOBETE MUSIC CO., INC.

75¢

MISCELLANEOUS

TOP ARTISTS

Artists with the most *Top 1000* ranked hits:

**# OF
HITS**

# OF HITS		
21	1.	**The Beatles**
19	2.	**Elvis Presley**
14	3.	**Michael Jackson**
13	4.	**Madonna**
12	5.	**The Supremes**
11	6.	**Mariah Carey**
11	7.	**Whitney Houston**
11	8.	**Paul McCartney/Wings**
10	9.	**George Michael/Wham!**
10	10.	**The Rolling Stones**
10	11.	**Stevie Wonder**
9	12.	**Bee Gees**
9	13.	**Elton John**
7	14.	**Phil Collins**
7	15.	**Daryl Hall & John Oates**
7	16.	**Janet Jackson**
6	17.	**Paula Abdul**
6	18.	**Pat Boone**
6	19.	**KC And The Sunshine Band**
6	20.	**Diana Ross**
5	21.	**Bon Jovi**
5	22.	**Boyz II Men**
5	23.	**John Denver**
5	24.	**Eagles**
5	25.	**The Everly Brothers**
5	26.	**The 4 Seasons**
5	27.	**Jackson 5**
5	28.	**Olivia Newton-John**
5	29.	**Prince**
5	30.	**Lionel Richie**
5	31.	**Barbra Streisand**

 # OF HITS: Artist's total hits making the *Top 1000*.

␐r artists with the same number of *Top 1000* hits, ties are broken by totaling the final ranking of each
␐p 1000 hit by these artists, and the artist with the highest ranking is listed first, and so on.

SONGS WITH MORE THAN ONE HIT VERSION

Songs which charted more than one version in the *Top 1000* :

Peak Position/Year (*Top 1000* Rank)

Butterfly
Andy Williams...1/'57 (236)
Charlie Gracie ....1/'57 (433)

Go Away Little Girl
Donny Osmond ....1/'71 (250)
Steve Lawrence......................................1/'63 (402)

I Heard It Through The Grapevine
Marvin Gaye...1/'68 (48)
Gladys Knight & The Pips ....2/'67 (954)

I'll Be There
Jackson 5 ....1/'70 (94)
Mariah Carey..1/'92 (429)

Lean On Me
Bill Withers ....1/'72 (296)
Club Nouveau ....1/'87 (534)

The Loco-Motion
Grand Funk ....1/'74 (511)
Little Eva ....1/'62 (741)

Please Mr. Postman
The Marvelettes ....1/'61 (689)
Carpenters ....1/'75 (857)

Venus
The Shocking Blue...................................1/'70 (628)
Bananarama...1/'86 (737)

When A Man Loves A Woman
Percy Sledge...1/'66 (542)
Michael Bolton ....1/'91 (609)

You Keep Me Hangin' On
The Supremes ....1/'66 (543)
Kim Wilde ....1/'87 (802)

Young Love
Tab Hunter...1/'57 (66)
Sonny James ....1/'57 (566)

SAME TITLES–DIFFERENT SONGS

The following *Top 1000* songs have the same title, but are not by the same composer(s). The artist with the highest ranked version is listed first, along with the year the title peaked:

All For Love
Bryan Adams/Rod Stewart/Sting ('94)
Color Me Badd ('92)

Best Of My Love
Emotions ('77)
The Eagles ('75)

Cherish
The Association ('66)
Kool & The Gang ('85)

Good Vibrations
Marky Mark & The Funky Bunch ('91)
Beach Boys ('66)

I'm Sorry
Brenda Lee ('60)
John Denver ('75)

Jump
Kris Kross ('92)
Van Halen ('84)

My Love
Paul McCartney & Wings ('73)
Petula Clark ('66)

One More Try
George Michael ('88)
Timmy -T- ('91)

Power Of Love
Celine Dion ('94)
Huey Lewis & The News ('85)

Venus
Frankie Avalon ('59)
The Shocking Blue ('70) and Bananarama ('86)

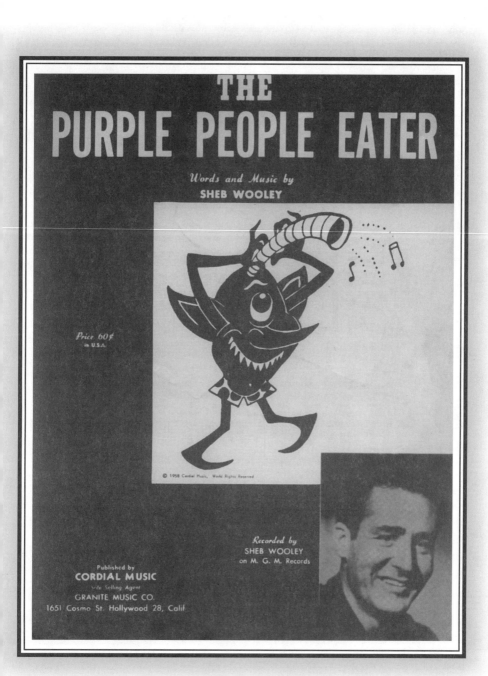

RE-CHARTED SINGLES

The *Top 1000* singles that hit the charts more than once:

RANK   PEAK POSITION/YEAR (WEEKS CHARTED)

20   **Rock Around The Clock**...*Bill Haley & His Comets*
1/'55(24); 39/'74(14)

22   **The Wayward Wind**...*Gogi Grant*
1/'56(28); 50/'61(9)

90   **All I Have To Do Is Dream**...*The Everly Brothers*
1/'58(17); 96/'61(2)

161   **Daydream Believer**...*The Monkees*
1/'67(12); 79/'86(4)

173   **Ode To Billie Joe**...*Bobbie Gentry*
1/'67(14); 54/'76(6)

195   **The Chipmunk Song**...*The Chipmunks*
1/'58(13); 41/'59(5); 45/'60(3); 39/'61(3); 40/'62(4)

197   **The Twist**...*Chubby Checker*
1/'60(18); 1/'62(21)

245   **Light My Fire**...*The Doors*
1/'67(17); 87/'68(6)

411   **Monster Mash**...*Bobby "Boris" Pickett & The Crypt-Kickers*
1/'62(14); 91/'70(3); 10/'73(20)

502   **At This Moment**...*Billy Vera & The Beaters*
79/'81(3); 1/'87(21)

551   **I Honestly Love You**...*Olivia Newton-John*
1/'74(15); 48/'77(9)

771   **Red Red Wine**...*UB40*
34/'84(15); 1/'88(25)

849   **When I'm With You**...*Sheriff*
61/'83(7); 1/'89(21)

889   **Louie Louie**...*The Kingsmen*
2/'63(16); 97/'66(2)

916   **Twist And Shout**...*The Beatles*
2/'64(11); 23/'86(15)

923   **Honky Tonk**...*Bill Doggett*
2/'56(29); 57/'61(10)

BREAKDOWN BY YEAR

Total records making the *Top 1000* year-by-year:

YR	TOP 1000	YR	TOP 1000
55	18	70	22
56	22	71	20
57	24	72	21
58	27	73	30
59	18	74	35
		75	37
Total	**109** (10.9%)	76	30
		77	32
		78	21
		79	24
		Total	**272** (27.2%)

YR	TOP 1000	YR	TOP 1000
60	22	80	19
61	23	81	24
62	20	82	21
63	25	83	22
64	25	84	22
65	26	85	28
66	30	86	31
67	21	87	31
68	20	88	33
69	21	89	33
Total	**233** (23.3%)	**Total**	**264** (26.4%)

YR	TOP 1000
90	26
91	29
92	19
93	13
94	12
95	15
96	8
Total	**122** (12.2%)

ALL THE HITS THAT

Only Joel Whitburn's Record Research Books List Every

Each book lists every record's significant chart data, such as peak position, debut date, peak date, weeks charted, label, record number and much more, all conveniently arranged for fast, easy reference. Most books also feature artist biographies, record notes, RIAA Platinum/Gold Record certifications, top artist and record achievements, all-time artist and record rankings, a chronological listing of all #1 hits, and additional in-depth chart information.

TOP POP SINGLES 1955-1993
Over 20,000 Pop singles — every "Hot 100" hit — arranged by artist. Features thousands of artist biographies and countless titles notes. 912 pages. $74.95 Hardcover / $64.95 Softcover.

POP ANNUAL 1955-1994
A year-by-year ranking, based on chart performance, of over 20,000 Pop hits. 880 pages. $69.95 Hardcover / $59.95 Softcover.

POP HITS 1940-1954
Compiled strictly from *Billboard* and divided into two easy-to-use sections — one lists all the hits artist-by-artist and the other year-by-year. Filled with artist bios, title notes, and many special sections. 414 pages. Hardcover. $44.95.

POP MEMORIES 1890-1954
Unprecedented in depth and dimension. An artist-by-artist, title-by-title chronicle of the 65 formative years of recorded popular music. Fascinating facts and statistics on over 1,600 artists and 12,000 recordings, compiled directly from America's popular music charts, surveys and record listings. 660 pages. Hardcover. $59.95.

TOP POP ALBUMS 1955-1996
An artist-by-artist history of the over 18,300 albums that ever appeared on *Billboard's* Pop albums charts, with a complete A-Z listing below each artist of <u>every</u> track from <u>every</u> charted album by that artist. 1,056 pages. Hardcover. $89.95.

TOP POP ALBUM TRACKS 1955-1992
An all-inclusive, alphabetical index of every song track from every charted music album, with the artist's name and the album's chart debut year. 544 pages. Hardcover. $34.95.

TOP POP ALBUM TRACKS 1993-1996
A 3 1/2-year supplement to the above Tracks book — alphabetically indexes over 21,000 tracks from the more than 1,600 albums that have appeared on The *Billboard 200* Pop Albums charts since 1992. 88 pages. Softcover. $14.95.

BILLBOARD HOT 100/POP SINGLES CHARTS:

THE EIGHTIES 1980-1989
THE SEVENTIES 1970-1979
THE SIXTIES 1960-1969
Three complete collections of the actual weekly "Hot 100" charts from each decade; black-and-white reproductions at 70% of original size. Over 550 pages each. Deluxe Hardcover. $79.95 each.

POP CHARTS 1955-1959
Reproductions of every weekly Pop singles chart *Billboard* published from 1955 through 1959 ("Best Sellers," "Jockeys," "Juke Box," "Top 100" and "Hot 100"). 496 pages. Deluxe Hardcover. $59.95.

BILLBOARD POP ALBUM CHARTS 1965-1969
The greatest of all album eras...straight off the pages of *Billboard*! Every weekly *Billboard* Pop albums chart, shown in its entirety, from 1965 through 1969. Black-and-white reproductions at 70% of original size. 496 pages. Deluxe Hardcover. $59.95.

TOP COUNTRY SINGLES 1944-1993
The complete history of the most genuine of American musical genres, with an artist-by-artist listing of every "Country" single ever charted. 624 pages. Hardcover. $59.95.

TOP R&B SINGLES 1942-1995
Revised edition of our R&B bestseller — loaded with new features! Every "Soul," "Black," "Urban Contemporary" and "Rhythm & Blues" charted single, listed by artist. 704 pages. Hardcover. $64.95.

EVER CHARTED

Title To Ever Appear On Every Major Billboard Chart.

TOP 10 CHARTS 1958-1995
A complete listing of each weekly Top 10 chart, along with each week's "Highest Debut" and "Biggest Mover" from the entire "Hot 100" chart, and more! 732 pages. Softcover. $49.95.

TOP ADULT CONTEMPORARY 1961-1993
America's leading listener format is covered hit by hit in this fact-packed volume. Lists, artist by artist, the complete history of *Billboard's* "Easy Listening" and "Adult Contemporary" charts. 368 pages. Hardcover. $39.95.

ROCK TRACKS
Two artist-by-artist listings of the over 3,700 titles that appeared on *Billboard's* "Album Rock Tracks" chart from March, 1981 through August, 1995 and the over 1,200 titles that appeared on *Billboard's* "Modern Rock Tracks" chart from September, 1988 through August, 1995. 288 pages. Softcover. $34.95.

BUBBLING UNDER THE HOT 100 1959-1985
Here are 27 years of *Billboard's* unique and intriguing "Bubbling Under" chart, listed by artist. Also features "Bubbling Under" titles that later hit the "Hot 100." 384 pages. Hardcover. $34.95.

BILLBOARD TOP 1000 x 5 1996 Edition
Includes five complete <u>separate</u> rankings — from #1 through #1000 — of the all-time top charted hits of Pop & Hot 100 Singles 1955-1996, Pop Singles 1940-1954, Adult Contemporary Singles 1961-1996, R&B Singles 1942-1996, and Country Singles 1944-1996. 288 pages. Softcover. $29.95.

TOP POP SINGLES CD GUIDE 1955-1979
This comprehensive guide tells you exactly where to find CD versions of past hits by your favorite Pop artists, with a complete listing of all 1955-1979 charted Pop records that are available on CD. 288 pages. Softcover. $24.95.

DAILY #1 HITS 1940-1992
A desktop calendar of a half-century of #1 pop records. Lists one day of the year per page of every record that held the #1 position on the Pop singles charts on that day for each of the past 53+ years. 392 pages. Spiral-bound softcover. $24.95.

BILLBOARD #1s 1950-1991
A week-by-week listing of every #1 <u>single</u> and <u>album</u> from *Billboard's* Pop, R&B, Country and Adult Contemporary charts. 336 pages. Softcover. $24.95.

MUSIC YEARBOOK 1995/1994/1993
A complete review of '95, '94 or '93 charted music — as well as a superb supplemental update of our Record Research Pop Singles and Albums, Country Singles, R&B Singles, Adult Contemporary Singles, and Bubbling Under Singles books. Various page lengths. Softcover. 1995 edition $34.95 / 1994 & 1993 editions $29.95 each.

MUSIC & VIDEO YEARBOOKS 1992/1991/1990/1989
Comprehensive, yearly updates on *Billboard's* major singles, albums and videocassettes charts. Various page lengths. Softcover. $29.95 each.

For complete book descriptions and ordering information, call, write, fax or e-mail today.

RECORD RESEARCH INC.
P.O. Box 200
Menomonee Falls, WI 53052-0200   U.S.A.
Phone: 414-251-5408 / Fax: 414-251-9452
E-mail: record@execpc.com

We're On The Internet — If you'd like to place an order electronically, simply use the convenient order form on our Web Site: **http://www.recordresearch.com.**

JOEL WHITBURN:
CHARTING HIS OWN COURSE

It was in 1970 that Joel Whitburn published the book bound to become a business.

The book–*Top Pop Records*–was a natural outgrowth of Joel's love of records and his penchant for filling file cards with *Billboard* chart data on each record he owned, the better to control his swelling collection.

This slim, 104-page volume–listing every single to ever appear on *Billboard's* Pop music charts from 1955-1969–was soon a big hit with the record and radio industries. And Record Research Inc. was born.

Since then, few, if any, individuals have taken the charts to heart quite like Joel Whitburn. In addition to *Top 1000 Singles 1955-1996*, "the world's foremost chart authority" has compiled well over 60 other books detailing the history and development of charted music from 1890 to the present.

Today, Joel's team of Record Researchers delves deeper into *Billboard's* charts than ever before, pouring out a steady stream of chart reference books widely noted for their detail, diversity, and painstaking accuracy. These books, currently used worldwide by collectors, disc jockeys, program directors, musicologists, artists and others, cover musical genres ranging from pop to country to R&B to modern rock and beyond.

As the largest privately-held record collection in the world, Joel's vast music library complete fills an environmentally-controlled underground vault adjacent to his Menomonee Falls, Wisconsin home. Here you'll find all the 300,000+ titles that ever appeared on *Billboard's* "Hot 100" and "Top Pop Albums" charts, along with a good share of the records that made *Billboard's* other charts.

And here, too, you'll find Joel Whitburn, collector extraordinaire, for whom charting a record's rise and fall has never lost its excitement or intrigue.